friends
of
Ishmael

bringing God's blessing to muslims

Luke Hollaway

Friends of Ishmael:
Bringing God's Blessing to Muslims
Copyright 2009 by Luke Hollaway

Book design by: qckslash

CSM Publishing
Email: direct@csm-publishing.com

09 10 11 12 13 5 4 3 2 1

ISBN 978-971-002-163-5

Printed in the Philippines

Table of Contents

Section 3

Section 4

Introduction

"We are the Kurds. We have no friends but the mountains!" This was the desperate cry of a Muslim group in the mountains of northern Iraq. The year was 1990. The world was preparing for war. Iraq had invaded her neighbor country, Kuwait. The world could not and would not sit by and do nothing.

However, three years before, the world either ignored or did not know about a greater tragedy than the invasion of Kuwait. It was what Saddam Hussein, the president of Iraq, called *Anfal*. *Anfal* was an attempt to destroy the Kurdish people. From 1987 to 1988, Saddam and his army destroyed nearly 4,500 Kurdish villages. As many as 180,000 people may have died in these *Anfal* campaigns. Hated by their neighbors, and freezing and dying in the mountains, the Kurds needed friends.

Chicquita Jean Hood nicknamed "Chickie" was born in rural Alabama and was raised on a small farm. She grew up knowing how to work and be responsible. She enjoyed water and snow skiing, hunting and camping. Her sister says, "She was always laughing and pulling practical jokes." Chickie's parents were very loving and caring. Her life was safe and secure. Chickie accepted Christ as her personal Savior when she was a young girl. She stayed involved in church, went on short-term mission trips and was involved in campus ministry in college. Chickie knew that Jesus was the Lord of her life, and He had the right to interrupt her life and change her plans.

Chickie had just graduated from college with a nursing degree and was working at a very good hospital. But when she heard the call from the Kurds, she could not say "no." Chickie went willingly to one of the mountain refugee camps in Northern Iraq and began showing the Kurds the love of Christ. She lived among them. She played with their children. She started learning their language. She took care of their sick. (They even started calling her "Dr. Chickie")

However, after only nine months, her life and ministry suddenly ended. Chickie was killed in a tragic auto accident. When news of her death reached the refugee camp where she had served and loved the Kurds, an amazing thing began to happen. All over the camp, signs and banners began to appear which said, "Chickie, a friend to the Kurds."

It is my purpose in writing this book that a new generation of young people would be challenged and inspired to become a friend to Muslims, bringing God's blessing to them through the gospel of Jesus Christ. I accept the idea that Muhammad sought to trace his family tree back to Abraham through Ishmael. Muslims all over the world believe they have descended either physically or spiritually from Hagar and Ishmael. Therefore, in the first section of the book, I have attempted to show the biblical background of God's love for Hagar and Ishmael, and why followers of Jesus should love and befriend Ishmael's descendants. Many times I will use the expression "sons of Ishmael" to refer to "Muslims."

Also, in this first section of the book, I tell the story of Muhammad, the early spread of Islam, and the Crusades of the Middle Ages. There is a 1,400-year history between Christians and Muslims. To be ignorant of this history is to risk making the same mistakes that early disciples made or to try and invent a methodology that has already been tried.

The second section of the book features some "old friends" of Ishmael. These missionaries were pioneers and trailblazers. Their lives and stories should not be forgotten. They serve as a testimony to God's faithfulness and a reminder of God's love for the sons of Ishmael. The worker among Muslims, at times, feels isolated and hopeless, seeing little results for his or her efforts. These stories should inspire and challenge the Muslim worker to continue. The lives of these pioneers should also encourage us that God is the one with the plan for reaching Muslims. His plan and activities among the sons of Ishmael have never stopped. Our generation is just one link in the never-ending chain of God's purpose to bring all people groups (including Muslims) into a relationship with Himself.

In the third section of the book, I tell the story of Franklin Graham, a modern day "Good Samaritan" to Muslims. The story is also told about two young ladies who dared to take the gospel of Jesus Christ into the heart of radical Islam. I conclude the third section of the book with stories of 21st century disciples who were willing to sacrifice everything to show the love of Christ to hurting Muslims and the story of a Filipino pastor who pioneered ministry to Muslims in the Philippines.

The final section of the book gives some practical helps in bringing God's blessing to Muslims. I have attempted to answer the following questions: What do Muslims believe? Are there different kinds of Muslims? Where do Muslims live? How can I bring the good news to my Muslim friends? What is the unfinished task?

The book closes with a final challenge. Is the spread of Islam unstoppable? Are Muslims unreachable? The answer to both of these questions is "NO!" The sons of Ishmael are becoming followers of Isa (Jesus) in numbers never before dreamed of in times past. Several testimonies of Muslim Background Believers (MBBs) have been included to challenge us to finish the task of taking the gospel to every unreached Muslim people group.

Section 1

1

God Sees, God Hears: The Story of Abraham, Hagar and Ishmael

On December 24, 2004, one of the greatest tragedies of human history took place. An earthquake caused a tsunami that swept across 8,000 kilometers of Asian and African coastlands. Approximately 500,000 people were instantly drowned. Most of the victims were Muslims, sons of Ishmael.

In response to this calamity, the news media skeptically asked, "Where was God in all of this?" However, one mission board leader asked, "Where were we (believers) that all these people were swept into eternity without knowing Christ?" Why is it that "in the last 25 years more than 100 times as many American Christians have gone to the Middle East to serve their country in a military capacity than have gone to the Middle East to serve the King of kings by proclaiming the gospel of peace?" (Love 2001:13) Why is it that "Iran has one missionary for every three million people while America has a full-time Christian worker for every 250 people? Why is it that Turkey has one missionary for every 270,000 people while Peru has one missionary for every

276 people?" (Hickman 2004:124-125) Why is it that there are over 3,000 missionaries and approximately five million evangelical believers in the Philippines, and the Muslims in that country are still unreached?

These numbers and percentages should bother us! Is it God's fault that so few followers of Jesus are working among the sons of Ishmael? Is it not God's will that they also receive peace and forgiveness and eternal life through Jesus Christ? Does God not see and hear the cries of the 1.3 billion Muslims?

Yes, God sees and hears! In response to the suffering of the Israelites when they were held as slaves in Egypt, God said to Moses, "I have indeed *seen* the misery of my people in Egypt. I have *heard* them crying out because of their slave drivers, and *I am concerned* about their suffering" (Exo. 3:7). Some may argue that God was concerned because these were the children of Israel, God's chosen people. Does God see and hear the sons of Ishmael?

Since Muslims trace their heritage back to Abraham, Hagar, and Ishmael, let us learn about God's relationship with these three. In the land of Ur, modern day Iraq, God chose a single man to be the means of blessing to every tribe in the world. "Leave your country, your people and your father's household and go to the land I will show you. I will make you into a great nation and I will bless you; I will make your name great, and you will be a blessing...and all peoples (tribes, languages) on earth will be blessed through you" (Gen. 12:1-3). Abram would become a great nation? How could this be? He was old. Very old! His wife could not have children and was past the age for childbearing.

However, God had promised. So they waited, and waited. Finally Sarai, Abram's wife, took matters into her own hands. She told Abram to sleep with her slave girl, Hagar. Abram agreed. Hagar probably had no choice. Hagar became pregnant. Sarai became jealous and angry. She said to Abram, "You are responsible for the wrong I am suffering" (Gen. 16:5). Abram told Sarai to do with Hagar whatever she wanted. Therefore, Sarai mistreated her and Hagar fled.

This should have been the end of the drama. Husband makes a mistake. Mistress runs away. However, God is love. He loved Abram. He loved Sarai. God also loved Hagar, and because of this love, He sent an angel to help her and rescue her. The angel said, "Go back to your mistress and submit to her" (Gen. 16:9). Then the angel added, "You are now with child and you will have a son. You shall name him Ishmael (God hears), for the LORD has heard of your misery. He will be a wild donkey of a man; his hand will be against everyone and everyone's hand against him, and he will live in hostility toward all his brothers" (Gen. 16:11-12). Then Hagar gave this name to the LORD who spoke to her; "You are the God who sees me" (Gen. 16:13). What an amazing story! God loves! God seeks! God sees! God hears!

Hagar returned home and it appeared that Ishmael would be the one through whom God's promises would be fulfilled. Abram loved Ishmael. However, when Abram was 99, and Sarai was 89, God appeared to them. He reconfirmed His covenant with Abram, giving circumcision as the sign of this special relationship. It should be noted at this point that Ishmael was also circumcised. He had a special relationship with God. He was included in God's family and was taught the ways of God. God then changed Abram's name to Abraham, which means, "Father of many." God told Abram that Sarai would have a child. They could not believe what they were hearing! After all these years, God had kept His promise!

Isaac was born. He was the child of promise, through whom the Savior of the world would come. It was through Isaac, not Ishmael, that God's nation would be established. Now Ishmael had a rival. He would lose everything because of Isaac. When Isaac was about two, Ishmael made fun of his little brother. Sarah overheard Ishmael's mockery and became very angry. Hagar and Ishmael were driven away. They became lost in the desert. With no food and water, they began to cry and sob and the Bible says, "God heard the boy crying, and the angel of God called to Hagar from heaven and said to her, 'What is the matter, Hagar? Do not be afraid; God has heard the boy crying as he lies there. Lift the boy up…for I will make him into a great nation'"(Gen. 21:17-18). If God cared so much for Hagar and Ishmael, then He also cares for the great nation of Muslims that came from them.

Yes, God sees! Yes, God hears the cries of the sons of Hagar today! They, too, are lost and dying! God desires that they be reconciled to Him through Jesus Christ. Jesus Christ is the true heir of Abraham, born through the family of Isaac. He was the long promised "seed of Abraham" (Gal.

3:16). The blessing of Abraham is only received through a relationship with Jesus Christ. "If you belong to Christ, then you are Abraham's seed, and heirs according to the promise" (Gal. 3:29).

Since God hears the cries of 1.3 billion Muslims and desires that they be reconciled with Him through Jesus Christ, why does Ishmael have so few friends among the followers of Jesus Christ? Why can't we hear Ishmael crying? I believe it is because we have allowed many other voices to drown out the call of God and the cries of Muslims. Some of these "voices" are lack of knowledge, pursuit of our own dreams and plans, universalism, prejudice, anger, and fear.

Lack of knowledge says, "I'm ok, but I don't know that you're not ok." *Pursuit of our own dreams* says, "I'm ok and I really don't care if you are not ok." *Universalism* says, "I'm ok and you are ok, so what is the problem?" This chapter will not deal with these problems per se, because it is my goal that by the time you have read the conclusion of this book, you will have enough knowledge to know what to do and where to do it, and enough inspiration and biblical background to give up your own dreams to do what you know needs to be done.

Prejudice and *anger* prevent many believers worldwide from loving Muslims and taking the gospel to them. The world, especially America, will never forget the images of the twin towers in New York City, burning and then crashing to the ground. Over 3,000 people were instantly killed. We remember those, who out of desperation, jumped to their deaths. We remember the firemen who willingly went into the buildings, knowing they would not come out alive. One of my most vivid memories is of President George Bush standing in the rubble promising Americans, and all those who stand for justice and freedom, "Whoever knocked down these buildings would hear from us real soon." I remember how good it felt to know that there would be retribution. I recently talked with someone whose American friend was killed in the war in Iraq. He confessed how, for several months, he began to hate all Muslims. These feelings of prejudice and anger are the same and even worse among Christians who have lived among and been at war with Muslims for years and sometimes decades.

How would Jesus respond today? He would say, "Love your enemies, do good to those who hate you, bless those who curse you, pray for those who mistreat you" (Lk. 6:27-28). He might also tell *The Good Samaritan* story as *The Good Muslim* story, showing that even those we hate are "our neighbor" (Lk. 10:25-37). Jesus would remind us that He washed His betrayer's feet (Jn. 13), prayed for those who crucified Him (Lk. 23:34), and commanded His disciples to take the gospel to *all people* (Mt. 28:18-20). If the apostle Paul could stand before us today, he would remind us that he became the apostle to the ones he once hated (Acts 9:15), and that we should never forget that our real enemy is Satan, not people (Eph. 6:12).

The son of a 21st century martyr gives us all an example to follow. He knelt down at the very spot where his father was killed by a Muslim extremist and committed himself to "pay them back for killing his father." However, he added, "I will not pay them back as the world would, but through love and by finishing the task of sharing the gospel of peace with all."

The voice of *fear* is another voice that keeps us from hearing the cries of Ishmael. Satan's strategy has never changed. He uses fear and intimidation to paralyze God's children. When Satan could not stop the first believers through threats (Acts 4:21), hypocrisy (Acts 5:1-10), or division (Acts 6), he began to kill and imprison them. The Bible says, "On that day a *great persecution* broke out against the church... Saul began to *destroy* the church. Going from house to house, he dragged off men and women and put them in prison" (Acts 8:1-3).

Satan thought he had solved the problem. Surely after seeing Stephen brutally killed (Acts 7) and witnessing the torture and imprisonment of family and friends, the believers would be afraid and stop preaching the gospel. But Satan underestimated these first believers because, "Those who had been scattered preached the word wherever they went" (Acts 8:4). In just a few years, the gospel had spread all throughout Judea and Samaria.

In the "Great Century" of missions (19th century) before the advancement of medical technology and transportation, the great fears were that of sickness and separation. Africa was known as the "missionary graveyard." In the Congo, in the 1800s, it is said that there were 20 missionary graves before there were 20 believers. Peter Cameron Scott was the founder of the African Inland Mission. He, along with seven others, arrived in East Africa in 1895. They envisioned establishing mission stations throughout the interior. There were no roads! For weeks, they hacked their way through the jungle, traveling only 200 miles. They opened their first station in Nzawe, known as the gateway to East Africa. Out of the original eight, four died and three were left crippled within the first five years.

When missionaries left their homeland to go as a missionary during this time period, it was very sad. They knew they were leaving and probably would never see their relatives again. Hudson Taylor recorded what he experienced when he left for China in 1853.

> My beloved mother had to come to see me off. Never shall I forget that day, nor how she went with me into the cabin (ship). We knelt down and prayed. Then notice was given that we must separate, and we had to say goodbye, never expecting to meet on earth again. For my sake, she restrained her feelings as much as possible. We parted and she went ashore giving me her blessing. I stood alone on the deck and she followed the ship as we moved toward the dock gates. As we passed through the gates, and the separation really started, never shall I forget the cry of anguish from that mother's heart. It went through me like a knife. I never knew so fully, until then, what "God so loved the world" meant. And I am quite sure my precious mother learned more of the love of God for the lost in that one hour than in all her life before. (Taylor 1927:187)

If you think that was an uncommon departure, read Adoniram Judson's words to his father-in-law. "I have now to ask whether you can agree to part with your daughter early next spring to see her no more in this world." (James 1998:33) During the 19th century, there were many followers of Jesus who said "no" to the call of God. They were afraid. The fear of sickness and separation kept them home.

Satan's time is short! He knows that when the gospel is preached to every tribe, then the end will come (Mt. 24:14). The "hidden tribes" of the world are no longer hidden. The advancement of medicine and technology has taken away the fears of sickness and separation. Messengers of the gospel can go anywhere in the world within a couple of days. Global economies and natural disasters prevent any country in the world from being completely "closed." Therefore, in Satan's mind, "The followers of Jesus must be stopped." Oppressive governments, severe persecution, and terrorism are now his weapons of fear. We must not allow these threats to make our world smaller than the one Jesus died for. We must not retreat and hide! We must explode the myth that the safest place is in the center of God's will. The Bible and history testify that those who advance the gospel into Satan's territory sometimes die. God doesn't call us to safety! God calls us to obedience!

The story is told of a believer in an Asian country who overcame his fear in order to become a friend to Ishmael.

Linaw is a village along the highway that has been known for ambush, hostage taking and armed conflict. But as Jose rode by this place on his motorcycle, the Lord began to put its people on his heart. The violent history of Linaw created great fear in Jose, but he had recently begun to understand through God's Word, that these Muslims were loved by God and in need of the gospel. He still could not bring himself to consider going into the village, but did pray faithfully each day as he quickly rode by. He prayed that God would send someone who would bring the gospel to these sons of Ishmael. One day as he rode past Linaw, there was a sudden downpour of rain and Jose had no choice but to stop at a bus stop by the side of the road. Fearfully, he entered the bus stop, all the while asking God what He was doing. Jose began to realize that his own prayer was being answered. God was sending someone to this unreached people group. God was sending Jose. As he waited for the rain to stop, some people from the village came into the bus stop and began to talk to Jose. His fear vanished as he began to make friends with them. Later, Jose began looking for ways to show God's love to this Muslim group and meet their needs, and as a result of Jose's friendship, three men from Linaw have accepted Jesus as their Messiah.

Let it not be said of this generation, "Where were you while Ishmael cried?"

God sees. God hears. Do you?

2

Muhammad (AD 570-632): The Beginning of Islam and the Crusades

In Chapter 1, the story of Abraham, Hagar and Ishmael was told so that you could see God's love for the ones Muslims claim as their physical (especially Arabs) and spiritual parents. Muhammad taught that these three and many other people from the Bible were Muslims, however, Islam as a religion did not start until 600 years after the time of Christ. Muhammad was its founder. Many Muslims will ask you, "What do you think of Muhammad?" This is a very hard question to answer, but as a follower of Jesus Christ, you need to know as much as you can about him and the early years of Islam. Also, some will ask, "Why is there so much hate between Muslims and Christians?" This chapter is about the life of Muhammad, the spread of Islam, and the Christian Crusades.

Muhammad was a man who lived about 1,400 years ago. He was born in the city of Mecca in Arabia (now Saudi Arabia) in AD 570. Mecca, at that time, was the center of pagan worship in Arabia. There were over 300 gods that were placed in the central temple of Mecca. Every year for four months, tribal warfare was stopped so the surrounding tribes could come and worship their gods. They would shave their heads, wear white robes, and make their pilgrimage to Mecca.

Muhammad's father, Abdullah, died a few months before Muhammad was born. When Muhammad was six years old his mother died. He was from the Hashemite clan of the Al Qu'raysh tribe. This tribe had learned the ways of the Bedouins. The Bedouins lived in tents and moved around the desert. They were well-known for being kind and merciful to the poor. After the death of his mother, Muhammad went to live with his grandfather and then his uncle, Abu Talib, a wealthy merchant.

Not much is known about Muhammad's early life. Islamic history records that when he was 12 he journeyed to Syria with his uncle. It is here that he may have been introduced to Christianity and Judaism (the religion of the Jews). He would have noticed their monotheism (worship of one god), which was so different from the polytheism (worship of many gods) in Mecca. Muhammad would have also noticed that the Christians and Jews had their own scriptures. Christianity had also spread to Arabia. However, during this time, there was much division and fighting among the Christians. The Church had lost its power. Muhammad probably worked as a shepherd when he was young. Later, he led caravans for rich merchants and was known to be trustworthy, kind, honest and hardworking.

When Muhammad was 25 years old, he went to work for Khadija, a wealthy widow. She was immediately attracted to him and asked him to marry her. Even though Khadija was 15 years older than Muhammad, they were happily married until her death, 25 years later. Muhammad traveled widely during this time, meeting Christians and Jews. He would have become familiar with some biblical stories. This too, had an influence on his views of religion.

Muhammad became more and more unhappy with the corruption among the merchants in Mecca. He began to spend many days by himself, praying and meditating. One of Muhammad's favorite places to go and meditate was in a cave at the base of Mount Hira, outside of Mecca. At the age of 40, Muhammad had his first experience, or revelation. He reported that the angel Gabriel (called Jibrail by Muslims) appeared to him. The angel held out a piece of cloth and ordered Muhammad to recite the words on it. Muhammad responded that he could not read or write. After this, the angel then recited the whole verse, "Recite, in the name of the Lord who created." Muhammad then understood that he was to repeat the words after the angel had first recited them.

He was very bothered by this first revelation. Muhammad confessed that he was not sure of the source of these revelations, whether they were from God or Satan. He thought he had been visited by an evil spirit or *Jinn* (in Islam, *Jinn* can be good or bad). After talking with his wife, Khadija, and a cousin named Waraqah, they convinced him that these revelations had come from God and that Allah had called him out. However, Muhammad remained in doubt for some time until he had another revelation which said the "Lord had not forsaken him." After this, the revelations came more frequently. It is said that, "sometimes he may have heard the words being spoken to him, but for the most part he seems simply to have 'found them in his heart.'" (McDowell 1983:379) These revelations continued for 22 years. The sayings were collected and written down. This is where the Qur'an came from.

It was during these first revelations that his wife and a few close friends came to believe in him as an "Apostle of God." They began to call themselves "Muslims," which means, "One who submits." (McDowell 1990:303) After three years of secrecy, Muhammad began his public preaching in AD 613. His message was to call the people of Mecca to worship the one God, Allah, to forsake idol worship, to prepare for the Day of Reckoning, to choose between heaven and hell, and to acknowledge him as a prophet. He preached for about six years without much opposition from the tribal leaders of the community. However, the leaders of the community began to worry because Muhammad was preaching against worshiping idols. What would happen if the idols were done away with? Mecca would lose money because no one would come to worship the many gods. For three years, persecution of Muhammad and his followers increased, until in June of AD 622, the tribal leaders plotted to kill Muhammad. Warned by some friends, Muhammad and Abu Bakr fled to the city of Medina, 300 kilometers away. This flight or Hijrah to Medina marked the beginning of Islam.

In Medina, Muhammad successfully united the warring tribal chieftains in the area and began to grow in power. It was here that his character began to change. After the death of his wife, he began to practice polygamy (having more than one wife). By the time of his death, only ten years later, he had 11 wives and two concubines. Even in these early years, *Jihad* (Holy War) was taking root. The once peaceful Muhammad was also becoming a man of war (Muslims today defend the early battles of Islam as being defensive). Muhammad, once the persecuted, was becoming the one who persecuted. He especially did not like the Jews because they rejected his prophethood. The Jewish tribes who resisted his authority and did not submit to him were attacked. All of the Jews in the Medina area, in time, were either deported or killed. Muhammad's goal was to create a Muslim state and community by fighting those who stood in his way.

Within a year of moving to Medina, Muhammad ordered the attack on an unarmed caravan going on pilgrimage to Mecca. This began a series of battles against the people of Mecca for the next eight years. Finally, in AD 630, Muhammad and his followers of about 10,000 were able to enter Mecca unopposed. He immediately went to the Ka'aba (the House or Temple, the place where the idols had been kept) and destroyed its idols and paintings. As soon as the shrine had been cleansed, Bilal, his first *mauzzin*, called the people to prayer. Muhammad called on the people of Mecca to become Muslims.

In the year AD 632, just ten years after his escape to Medina, Muhammad died of a mysterious illness. He was 62 years old. Muhammad was buried in his house and a mosque was built around it. This mosque can still be visited in Medina. Throughout his life, he had shown unshakable commitment to his calling, was courageous in battle, and was known to be a powerful speaker and peacemaker between warring tribes. He was known to be committed to prayer, giving of alms, fasting, and generosity.

The early history of Islam, after the death of Muhammad, is one of glorious wars, victories, defeats, division, hatred, and incredible expansion of the Islamic religion through military conquest. Because Muhammad did not appoint someone to take over after his death, there was much fighting over this position. Should Islam be led by a direct descendant of Muhammad? This question later split the Islam religion into two major divisions known as the Shiah Muslims and the Sunni Muslims. These two divisions will be discussed later in the book.

As Islam spread, the new territories were controlled by a series of leaders known as Khalifs. These leaders had both political and religious power. The first four Khalifs were known as "Rightly Guided Khalifs." They ruled from AD 633 to 661. During this time, Islamic armies spread the new religion across all of the Middle East, Egypt, and Iran.

The Umayyad Khalifs were the next to rule the Islamic empire. They moved the base of operation to Damascus, Syria. For the next 90 years, these rulers expanded Islamic territory to the east, conquering Afghanistan, Pakistan, and parts of northern India. China's massive army was able to stop their advancement at its borders. To the west, the Umayyads took over the rest of North Africa and began their invasion of Europe through Morocco and Spain. They conquered most of Spain and were finally defeated in France in AD 732 by Charles Martel, the grandfather of Charlemagne, the first Holy Roman emperor.

Although the Umayyads were successful in spreading Islam to many new territories, they were not very popular in Arabia. Rebellions and civil war broke out, and in AD 749, most of the Umayyad family was killed, thus ending their rule. The Abbasids took control and ruled until 1258. The first few Khalifs in this dynasty were strong and had worldwide influence. Abu Ja'far al-Mansur, in AD 762, established a new capital in Baghdad. He built many fountains and gardens. However, his greatest achievement was the building of the Dar al-Hikma (House of Wisdom), which was a combination library and translation center.

The most famous of the Abbasid Khalifs was Harun ar-Rashid who ruled from AD 786 to 809. During his rule, people from all over the world came to visit Baghdad bringing their goods; metal work from Spain, perfumes from Egypt, spices from India and silk from China. The House of Wisdom became the world's most important center of learning.

During the ninth century, Turkish people from Central Asia migrated to the Middle East. Thousands of Turkish warriors joined the Islamic armies and their officers gradually took over the political power. This was the beginning of the decline of this great Abbasid dynasty until finally, in AD 1248, Baghdad was invaded and defeated by the Mongolian empire.

At the first of this great Islamic expansion, "freedom of religion" was granted by the Muslim conquerors. Conversions to Islam by Christians and Jews was allowed and encouraged. Conversion from Islam to Christianity was punishable by death. This is still practiced today in some Islamic countries. The following were the choices of the defeated lands as Islam expanded: (Nehls 1996:14)

1. The acceptance of Islam, in which case the conquered became enfranchised citizens of the Muslim state.
2. The payment of poll-tax (*Jizra*) by which people of the book, i.e. Jews and Christians obtained "protection," becoming 'Zimmis.'
3. Death by sword to those who would neither accept Islam nor pay the poll tax.

However, in the 11th century, churches were destroyed and Christians and Jews alike were killed. Finally, Muslims destroyed the Church of the Resurrection over the sites of Christ's crucifixion and burial in Jerusalem. For four centuries before Islam, this church had been the most venerated and visited place of early Christians. This began a movement in Christian history called the Crusades. The Crusades were a series of military expeditions made by Christians from Western Europe to take control back from the Muslims in the city of Jerusalem and the surrounding area known as the Holy Land. The first Crusade was announced in 1095, and these continued (eight crusades in all) for the next 200 years, causing much pain and suffering and loss of life for both Christians and Muslims. The Crusades not only failed in their purpose to take back the Holy Land, but they also deepened the gulf that still exists today between Christians and Muslims.

In closing, these questions must be asked:

- What would the world look like today if Muhammad would have had a true Christian friend when he was searching for truth?
- What would the world look like if the Church had been prepared spiritually to answer the Islamic expansion?
- What would the world look like if Christians then had responded in love and in the power of the Holy Spirit, instead of using the cross as a symbol of war and revenge?

Islam's goal is world conquest, but the battle we fight is not with the weapons of the world. God's kingdom is established as we wage war on the spiritual forces of evil (the Devil and demons) and wage peace on the sons of Ishmael, through telling the good news of Abraham's blessing.

Section 2
Old Friends of Ishmael

3

Raymund Lull (1232-1325): The First Friend of Ishmael

The Crusades (1095-1291), which were an effort by the Christians to take back Muslim-held lands, cannot be considered missions according to our biblical understanding of the word. As discussed in the last chapter, the hatred and suspicion these wars created between Muslims and Christians continue to this day. During this period of Crusades, there were only two individuals who seemed to understand the will of God toward Muslims. The great monastic founder Francis of Assisi and the Spanish nobleman, Raymund Lull, attempted to preach a gospel of peace and love instead of war.

Francis of Assisi (1182-1226) was born into wealth. He had little education. As a young person, he lived a worldly life. However, at the age of 23, after being held as a prisoner of war for one year, he began his service to God. Francis's changed life and his giving to the poor made his father angry. Francis's father threatened to take away his inheritance and took Francis to court. It is recorded that Francis publicly gave up his inheritance to follow the will of God. Francis even took off the clothes his father had bought him and walked out of the courtroom naked!

For the next three years, Francis took care of outcasts and lepers. During this time, he also restored the ruined chapel of Santa Maria degli Angeli. In 1208, one day during Mass, he heard a call telling him to go into all the world, and according to the text of Matthew 10:5-14, to possess nothing, but to do good everywhere. That same year, Francis began preaching. He gathered around him 12 disciples. These 12 became the first order of the Franciscan monks.

During this time, there was still much support for the Crusades. In spite of this, Francis suggested that Muslims should be won by love instead of fighting. Francis's first two attempts to evangelize ended in failure. However, in 1219, he went to Egypt, and in spite of the language barrier, Francis made an attempt to witness to the Sultan. Though there is no evidence that the Sultan was converted, Francis's example encouraged others to reach out to Muslims in love; among them was Raymund Lull.

Raymund Lull was born in 1232 into a wealthy Roman Catholic family on the island of Majorca, off the coast of Spain. As a young man, he went to Spain and served in the court of the king. While there he lived a very immoral life. However, he was very intelligent and was recognized as an excellent writer.

In his early thirties, Lull returned home to Majorca. During this time, according to Samuel Zwemer, he was "born again." Lull came to know the Lord and His will through a series of visions. He experienced his first vision one evening while composing a vulgar or worldly song. Suddenly he saw Jesus hanging on the cross, His blood trickling from His hands and brow. Moreover, Jesus sadly looked at him. Though convicted by the vision, Lull continued with his songwriting the next week. But again the vision appeared. This time, overcome with guilt because of his sins, he forsook his wealth and prestige and committed his life to Jesus Christ. He immediately became a monk.

In those days, it was common for people who were "totally committed to God" to go and live in a monastery where they could spend all their time praying, fasting and meditating on God's Word. Monks believed that the way to show one's love for God was living as a recluse (one who lives by himself), wholly separated from the temptations of the world.

Through another vision, Lull became aware of his responsibilities to those around him. In his book, *The Tree of Love*, he relates the vision that became his missionary call.

> While in the forest alone with God, far removed from worldly distractions, he meets a pilgrim, who, on learning of Lull's chosen vocation, scolds him for his self-centeredness and challenges him to go out into the world and bring others the message of Christ. It was the vision that caused Lull to leave the monastery and go as a foreign missionary to the Saracens (peoples of North Africa), the most hated and feared enemies of the Christians of that day. He wrote, "I see the Knights (warriors of the Crusades) going to the Holy Land beyond the seas, thinking they can take back the Holy Land by force, but in the end, all are destroyed. It seems to me the best way to conquer the Holy Land ought to be attempted by love and prayers and the pouring out of tears and blood." (Tucker 1983:54)

Following the vision, Lull devoted much of his time for the next nine years to Arabic language study. Now past the age of 40, he began his missionary career. He wrote about what following Christ cost him personally. "I had a wife and children; I was fairly rich; I had been successful. All these things I gladly gave up for the sake of preaching the gospel to the unreached." (Tucker 1983:54) Lull set aside enough money for his family and the remainder he gave to the poor.

Lull's missionary strategy had three parts: apologetical, educational, and evangelistic. He developed logical arguments for convincing Muslims of the truth of Christianity; he established missionary colleges; and he himself went to preach to the Muslims.

Lull's contribution as a Christian apologist to Muslims was incredible. He wrote 60 books on theology, many of them written to convince Muslim scholars of the truth of Christianity. The theme of his arguments mostly centered on the Godhead. His mission as he saw it was to persuade Muslim scholars and leaders by open debate of the truths of the Trinity, incarnation, death and resurrection of Jesus.

According to Lull's account, after immediately arriving in a new place he would boldly challenge the Muslims to compare their religion with Christianity. One of his arguments in these debates, as Zwemer relates, was to present the Ten Commandments as the perfect law of God, and then showing from their own books that Muhammad violated every one of the laws. In these debates, Lull would also teach the seven cardinal virtues and seven cardinal sins, showing that Islam had no virtues and was full of sins.

As can be expected, Lull's "New Method," as he called it, was not very successful. On his first missionary journey to Tunis, after a public debate, he was immediately thrown into prison, later stoned, and ordered out of the country. Fifteen years later, on his second missionary journey to Bugia, Lull's public debating did not last long. He was sent to prison and for six months, his captors "tempted him with all of the pleasures of Islam." Again, he was sent home to Europe. Though Lull claimed to reach out to Muslims in love, his message and method was often very offensive and embittered many Muslims toward Christianity.

Lull probably had his greatest impact on Muslim evangelism in the area of education. He viewed monasteries as a good training ground for missionaries. He traveled widely, trying to get support for his cause from church and political leaders. He was able to get the support from King James II of Spain and established a monastery on his home island. The curriculum included the Arabic language and the geography of missions. This may have been the first training school for Muslim ministry.

Lull's dream was to establish training centers for Muslim ministry all over Europe. When he visited Rome on several occasions, his ideas were made fun of or ignored by the Pope and Cardinals. However, in spite of the lack of support for his vision, he was still able to establish several missionary-oriented monasteries. His greatest victory in the area of education came at the Council of Vienna, when he convinced church leaders to have Arabic offered in the European universities.

Even at the age of 75, Lull was still traveling, writing, lecturing, and teaching Arabic in the universities. Most people at this age would be thinking of retirement, but Lull had other plans. His ambition was to die as a missionary, not as a teacher of philosophy. In Lull's writings we read, "Men are going to die, O Lord, from old age, etc; but if it be Your will, Your servant does not want simply to die; he would prefer to die showing love, even as You were willing to die for me." (Piper 1993:109) Nate Saint, missionary martyr, expressed this same commitment.

> The Lord tells us that he that loves his life—we might say that he is selfish with his life—shall lose it. People who do not know the Lord ask why in the world we waste our lives as missionaries. They forget they too are expending their lives. They forget that when their lives are over, they will have nothing of eternal significance to show for the years they have wasted. Some might say, isn't it too great a price to pay? When missionaries consider themselves—their lives before God— they consider themselves expendable. Isn't the price small in the light of God's infinite love? Those who know the joy of leading a stranger to Christ and those who have gone to tribes, who have never heard the gospel, are gladly willing to give up their lives. And they count it all joy. (Hitt 1959:142-143)

Having been imprisoned and stoned in Tunis in 1291, and then imprisoned again in 1307, at the age of 80, Lull was ready for his third missionary journey. He returned to Tunis and was granted freedom by the authorities. Some Muslims became followers of Jesus. Desiring to spend time with some of his disciples in Bugia, he went there, and for almost a year, secretly taught them. Zwemer records,

> Tired of being alone, and longing for martyrdom, he came out to the open market and presented himself to the people as the same man whom they had expelled from their town. Lull stood before them and threatened them with divine wrath if they still continued in their sins. He pleaded with love, but spoke plainly the whole truth. The result can be easily anticipated. Filled with hate at his boldness, and unable to reply to his arguments, the people grabbed him, and dragged him out of town; there by the command or at least the permission of the king, he was stoned. He died on June 30th, 1315. (Piper 1993:110)

Some have said that Lull's "longing for martyrdom" was not the best method he could have used to try and reach the Muslims with the gospel. He should have stayed and worked secretly with his disciples. Mission strategies today emphasize safety instead of boldness, and secrecy instead of publicly proclaiming Christ. Of course, God wants us to use wisdom to be most effective in reaching the most resistant peoples, but maybe what the Church needs today are more martyrs like Raymund Lull.

George Otis, at the second Lausanne Congress on World Evangelism in Manila in 1989, asked these questions:

> "Is our failure to succeed in Muslim countries because of the absence of martyrs? Can a covert (secret) church grow in strength? Does a young church need martyr models?" Otis states further, "Should the Church in politically and socially hard circumstances remain secret to avoid persecution by those

hostile to Christianity? Or would more open confrontation, even if it resulted in Christian martyrs, be more likely to lead to evangelistic breakthroughs? Islamic fundamentalists claim that their spiritual revolution continues because of the blood of martyrs. Is Christianity's failure to thrive in the Muslim world due to the lack of Christian martyrs? And can the Muslim community really believe the message of a church in hiding? The question is not whether it is wise at times to keep worship and witness secret, but rather how long this may continue before we are guilty of hiding our light under a bushel...The record shows that from Jerusalem and Damascus to Ephesus and Rome, the apostles were beaten, stoned, and imprisoned for their witness." (Piper 1986:228)

Lull's life and work are testimony to the power of true Christianity to shine, even in the darkest periods of church history. Francis of Assisi and Raymund Lull were rare indeed! For several hundred years before and after their lives, there were no other well-known friends of Ishmael. Only now are followers of Jesus beginning to look beyond fear and prejudice to follow Lull's example. The greatest advancement of the gospel among Muslims has taken place in the last half of the 20th century. It is time! God is moving! God is calling this generation to catch a vision and "turn away from self-centeredness," and go out into the Muslim world and bring them the message of Christ.

4

Henry Martyn (1781-1812): The Father of Protestant Missions to Muslims

Few missionaries have accomplished so much in such a short time as Henry Martyn. He was a scholar, a linguist (person who studies and knows many languages), and a friend to Muslims in India and Iran. He has been called by some the "Father of Protestant Missions to the Muslims." In just seven years, he translated the New Testament into the Urdu language (which is spoken in India and modern day Pakistan), Arabic, and Persian. He died of tuberculosis at the age of 31.

Henry Martyn was born in Cornwall, England in 1781. His mother died when he was two years old. His father was the office manager of a mining company and provided well for Martyn and his sisters. Spiritually, the family was influenced by the sermons and songs of the famous evangelists, John and Charles Wesley. Martyn attended a very good grammar school and at the age of 16, entered Cambridge University. Four years later, he graduated with the highest honors in mathematics. A year later, he won first prize for a paper written in Latin.

He had turned his back on God during his youth. But even with all his academic achievements, he was not satisfied. After being welcomed as a hero in his hometown, he still had these words to say: "I obtained my highest wishes, but was surprised to find that I had grasped a shadow." (Page 2003:26) Martyn, during this time, was challenged by a sermon entitled, "Do not seek great things for yourself." The death of his father, the reading of the Scriptures, the prayers of his sister, and the counsel of a godly minister influenced him to surrender his life to Jesus Christ.

Not long after his conversion, Martyn began to hear stories about William Carey, the Baptist missionary who had sailed for India in 1793. Martyn's pastor spoke enthusiastically about the progress being made in translating the Bible. Martyn also started reading books about David Brainerd, the dedicated man who had preached to the North American Indians. Brainerd had worn himself out in the service for God and died at the age of 32. Martyn wanted to be like Brainerd: holy and totally committed to God. He began to pray that God would send out more missionaries, until finally he asked himself the question, "Why not me?" In 1802, Martyn made the decision to forsake a life of honor and comfort to become a foreign missionary.

Like his hero David Brainerd, Martyn spent many hours each day in reading the Scriptures, prayer, and devotion to God. He also began the practice of writing his thoughts, struggles, prayers, and experiences down in a notebook for the purpose of becoming more holy. His *Journal and Letters* continue to encourage people today because they show that the missionary is a normal person with problems and struggles.

Once he wrote, "Let me forget the world and be swallowed up in a desire to glorify God." (Tucker 1983:133) In his effort to be more dedicated and to prepare himself for the hardships of the mission field, Martyn began practicing self-denial. For example, he would read or eat his meals standing at a distance from the fire, even though it was below zero degrees. Celibacy, or remaining single, was another aspect of his self-denial. He was thankful he was "delivered from all desires for the comforts of married life," preferring a "single life in which are much greater opportunities for heavenly mindedness." (Tucker 1983:133) But that was before he fell in love with Lydia Grenfell. She became his one "idolatrous affection" which, more than anything, distracted him from his single-minded goal of going to work in India.

In the spring of 1805, Martyn, 24 years old, was ordained as an Anglican minister. The following month he was appointed as a chaplain to the East India Company. At this time in history, England was ruling in India with the East India Company controlling all trade in the area. The company had detachments of soldiers in different parts of the Empire to guard their interests; thus, Martyn was assigned to pastor the soldiers, employees, and families of the East Indian Company. It was also a well-known fact that the Company opposed the preaching "to the natives." However, Martyn was going with the vision of working and living among the Indians. He left England in the summer of 1805 and arrived in Calcutta on May 16, 1806. The first day ashore, he found William Carey.

He had left Lydia behind wanting to prove his reliance on God alone, but after only two months in India, he wrote and proposed to her. Sure of her positive response, he made plans for her arrival to India. He waited 15 months for her reply! His journal entry on October 24, 1807 reads:

> An unhappy day; received at last a letter from Lydia, in which she refuses to come, because her mother will not give her permission. Grief and disappointment threw my soul into confusion at first; but gradually my eyes were opened. I agree with her, that it would not be for the glory of God, nor could we expect his blessing, if she acted in disobedience to her mother. (Piper 1993:73)

For five years, he waited and hoped that Lydia would change her mind. Many letters were sent across the thousands of miles between India and England. In spite of Martyn's deep love for Lydia, he did not let this romance keep him from doing God's will. How many young people have been turned away from a call to missions because of a relationship? A young man asked me one time, "Is it okay if I tell God I will not be a missionary unless I am married?" "Of course it is not okay," I said. "You can tell God of your desire to marry, but if God has called you to go, then you must be obedient and go whether you are married or not."

For four years, Martyn served at military posts, preaching to both Europeans and Indians, establishing schools, and at the same time translating the New Testament into Urdu, Persian, and Arabic. Although most of his time was spent alone with native language helpers, he did enjoy the company of different Englishmen and high-ranking officials. He was comfortable talking with beggars as well as governors and ambassadors. He could talk with intelligence with any scholar, but also enjoyed playing and laughing with children.

During these first four years in India, his journals reveal much of his burden for the lost, work ethic, faith in God, and victories for the kingdom of God. Concerning his burden for the lost, he said, "Looking around this country and reflecting upon its condition is enough to overwhelm the mind of the minister or missionary. When once my mouth is opened, how shall I ever dare to be silent?" (Page 2003:83) "While Satan is so active in destroying their souls, the servants of God cannot be lukewarm." (Page 2003:78) With regard to his work ethic, which led to his early death, he wrote, "What a wicked person I am if I do not work from morning until night in a place where, in whole provinces, I seem to be the only light." (Page 2003:86) In one of his letters home he admitted, "I work as hard as we ever did for our degrees at Cambridge. I have read and corrected the copies of my Urdu Testament so often that my eyes ache." (Page 2003:91)

Any missionary, who spends time in the middle of Satan's territory, establishing the Kingdom of God, faces times of discouragement and despair. Every need cannot be met. Every person cannot be reached. Sometimes there is no success or response. In these times, the missionary needs faith in an unchanging God who rewards obedience. Martyn wrote "Let me labor for fifty years, amidst scorn and without seeing one soul converted, still it shall not be worse for my soul in eternity, or even worse for it in time. Though the heathen rage, the Lord Jesus who controls all events is my Friend, my Master, my God, my All." (Page 2003:94)

His faith made him fearless in the face of death. One particular time when death seemed sure he wrote, "And when we have left this world, there will be no more sorrow, nor sighing, nor any pain." (Page 2003:126) In fact, his journals record him speaking often of death. He believed he would die young, as had his hero, David Brainerd. Because he was not afraid of death, he was not afraid of men. He was free to be a friend, speak the truth, and let God worry about his future, whether he lived or died.

Rich Mullins, a Christian singer who died in 1997, often sang and spoke about death. He knew that there was only one thing sure in life and that was death. This understanding of death (dying in Christ) set him free to live. He was no longer afraid of failure. He could take risks. Understanding that life was short also freed him to love. This realization made each day important. Rich told audiences "Love each other as much as you can right now because this may be the last day you have to love each other." (Smith 2000:231)

It is a hard lesson to learn that people cannot be hustled or forced into the kingdom of God, especially when one is working in a "hard field." Jesus compared the kingdom to leaven and seed; things that work slowly and out of sight. We long to see results and when these results do not come, we are tempted to conclude that our efforts were in vain. While ministering to beggars and orphans in the city of Cawnpore, India, Martyn wondered whether he had done any good. What he never knew was on the first Sunday there had been a group of rich young men passing by. They were curious about the strange meeting. One, a Muslim professor who knew both Persian and Arabic, heard enough to want to learn more. He approached Martyn's language helper and became employed as a copier of the Persian New Testament. He was given a copy of the complete New Testament to take to the bookbinder. He kept it long enough to read it all before passing it on, and he believed what he read. He was later baptized in 1811 and became a preacher and well-known Christian leader.

Four years in India had produced much fruit in translation work, but the busy work schedule and climate of Central India had nearly killed Martyn. With the Persian New Testament needing many revisions, Martyn left on a sea voyage to Persia, hoping to restore his health, and at the same time, complete the translation work. Like the apostle Paul, ever wanting to go where the gospel had not been preached, Martyn dreamed of going also to Damascus, Baghdad, and into the very heart of Arabia.

With a letter of introduction from a high-ranking diplomat, Martyn went to Shiraz, the city of poets and learning; the center of Persia's culture. He was received warmly by the leading citizen of the city and given a room. For over a year, Martyn was free to translate and receive guests and scholars from this Muslim city. Some came with a genuine desire to learn more of the Christian faith, seeking proof for the religion of Christ; others came only to argue, and some simply to scoff. But they came! One young scholar, who on his first visit came to taunt, found his attitude changing as he listened to the calm reasoning of this man of God. This scholar returned many times until he believed in Christ. It is said that as Martyn was met with verbal abuse about Christ, his eyes would fill with tears. Tears, love, and friendship are what God uses to reach sons of Ishmael.

With the New Testament complete and his health broken, Martyn began an overland trip of 2,000 kilometers to England. The trip was too much for his weak body. He died in Tokat, Asia Minor in the fall of 1812. His Persian New Testament was published in 1815 and then revised and republished in 1816. When the Shah of Persia received a copy, he was delighted and publicly expressed his approval, recommending it as a book to read from beginning to end.

Henry Martyn will be remembered as a linguist and translator. Through his work, he was able to place portions of the Scriptures into the language of one-fourth of the entire population of the world. (Page 2003:157) He was a forerunner, a pioneer. Many young people followed his example of commitment and zeal by going to the hard-to-reach places of the world. H.B. Dehqani-Tafti, former Presiding Bishop of the

Church in Jerusalem and the Middle East (1976-1986) and first Anglican Bishop in Iran said, "Without his tireless efforts the Church in Iran would probably not have taken root, and people like myself might not have become Christians." (Finnie 8) He was a seeker after God and a seeker of lost souls. Martyn had written in his journal, "Now let me burn out for God." In his love for Muslims, he had done just that.

5

Ion Keith-Falconer (1856-1888): Missionary to Arabia

Hebrews chapter 11 is a list of heroes of the faith. Some of them, by their faith, saw results and experienced victories. These heroes prayed and God answered immediately and miraculously. Others, by faith, heard God speak, stepped out in obedience, and "did not receive the things promised; they only saw them and welcomed them from a distance" (Heb. 11:13). In other words, they prayed and there was "no answer." They "went out" and there were "no results." These heroes obeyed the Great Commission and were met with death.

We like the stories that end well. We want our Christian life to be like the typical movie where the boy wins zthe girl and the star of the movie never dies. But we know that in real life, the story doesn't always end well. Elisabeth Elliot, in her book *These Strange Ashes*, tells how the first years of her missionary career ended in "failure." But after many years of thinking about those early trials (which included the violent death of her husband) she concluded, "God's story never ends in ashes."

In other words, when it looks like all is gone or we have failed, God is still in control and He is working. She reminds us that the kingdom of God is like "leaven and seed. Things work slowly and out of sight. We long for visible evidence of our effectiveness, and when we do not see any evidence, we are tempted to conclude that our efforts never had anything to do with the kingdom." (Robson 1922:135) Some things can only bear fruit after they have died. Jesus said, "Unless a kernel of wheat falls to the ground and dies, it remains a single seed. But if it dies, it produces many seeds" (Jn. 12:24).

Ion Keith-Falconer has been forgotten by this generation, but he is remembered by God as a hero of the faith. He was a friend of Muslims that took the gospel to southern Arabia. He was a world Christian that gave up status and prestige to go to the unreached. His ministry and life was short. His story did not end well. He was only 31 years old when he died. He did not see many results, but he was obedient. He died, yes, but he died in battle facing forward.

Keith-Falconer was born on July 5, 1856, in Scotland. Scotland is a part of the United Kingdom on the island of Great Britain. He was born into nobility. The Keith-Falconer family could trace their genealogy back to the 11th century. It is well documented that Ion Keith-Falconer had past relatives who were war heroes, members of Parliament, participants in the Protestant Reformation, and one relative who founded a famous college. Keith-Falconer's father was the Earl of Kintore. An "earl" was an official of the government who ruled over a municipality.

Keith-Falconer not only had the privilege of being born into wealth and nobility, but his parents were also committed Christians. They were a part of the Free Church of Scotland. The Free Church of Scotland had been established only a few years before because the believers wanted separation of church and state. They did not believe that the government had the right to make decisions regarding the doctrines, disciplines, and government of the church.

It is recorded that, even at an early age, Keith-Falconer was sensitive to spiritual things. When he was seven years of age, he began to visit neighbors and read the Bible to them. He often gave money and food to the poor. When he was 11, he was sent to preparatory school and at 13, was accepted into Harrow School (high school). Harrow School is still in existence today in London, England. It is a very famous school. At this school, Keith-Falconer received awards in his studies of German and mathematics. He also began to study shorthand, and would later become an expert in this style of writing.

Keith-Falconer attended Cambridge University, the second oldest university in the United Kingdom. At Cambridge he studied theology, Hebrew, and Greek. Not only was Keith-Falconer a brilliant student, but he also became one of the "best cyclists in England." He broke many of the professional and amateur records. One of his greatest accomplishments was his bicycle trip from Land's End (southwest tip of England) to John o' Groats (northeast tip of Scotland). This trip had never been made by bicycle. He covered a distance of 994 miles in 13 days and 45 minutes. That time is not very good with today's bicycles and roads, but for his day it drew national attention. (It was not until 1885 that a bicycle was created with equal-sized wheels, and was driven by a chain. It was not until 1888 that air-filled tires were created.) Because of his ability and respect, Keith-Falconer was elected president of the London Bicycle Club for nine years.

It is amazing that with all of his studies, Keith-Falconer still found time to be involved in many ministries while attending Cambridge University. One of these ministries was helping to start a church in a nearby district where hundreds were reached with the gospel. Another ministry was a partnership with a Mr. Charrington who gave up a great fortune to follow Christ. Mr. Charrington and Keith-Falconer started a mission. One of the results of the work was that a gang of young thieves was broken up, and God began to bring in a harvest. The work, which began in a barn, grew until an assembly hall was built which could hold 4,300 people. Keith-Falconer was also involved in displaying Scripture texts and religious signs in public places. Lastly, during the winter of 1879, many people were out of work and were starving. Keith-Falconer describes the situation, "Hundreds of men were waiting daily at the docks in the hope of a job, but rarely found one. The result was starvation. Starving men were found in several instances eating orange peels picked up from the road. In a period of six weeks, 20,000 meals were given and over 300 families were helped every week in their houses." (Robson 1922:46-47)

After graduation, Keith-Falconer continued his studies. His opportunities, offers, and successes continued. He studied

German and was offered a position with a general in the military. He also became fluent in Arabic while living in Egypt. In 1882, Keith-Falconer published a book, and in 1883, became a lecturer in Hebrew at Cambridge. In 1884, he became an assistant in the theology department. Also that year, he was married.

Keith-Falconer had it all! He was 28 years old. He was wealthy, educated, successful, and a famous athlete. He had every door of opportunity open for him. He could have chosen a career in education or politics, but he began to feel a higher calling. For some time, he had felt that he must "devote his life to religious work." However, it was near the end of 1884 that he began to seriously consider giving his life to be a foreign missionary.

During this time, one influence on Keith-Falconer's life was a biography about the life of John Wilson. John Wilson had been a missionary doctor in India, and had sacrificed greatly to help the poor in Bombay. Another influence on Keith-Falconer was his friendship with the famous C.T. Studd and the events surrounding the calling out of the "Cambridge seven." In 1882, the American evangelist, D.L. Moody visited Cambridge University. Moody's one-week evangelistic meetings brought many people to faith in Christ. At the same time, there was growing interest in a new mission, the China Inland Mission, recently founded by J. Hudson Taylor. Moody's revival and Taylor's call that a "thousand a day were dying in China without ever hearing the gospel," resulted in seven outstanding students volunteering to go to China.

Before leaving for China, the "Cambridge seven" traveled all over England and Scotland, visiting campuses and churches. They preached the gospel and presented the great needs of the world for missionaries. Keith-Falconer and his wife were present at the commissioning services held for C.T. Studd at Cambridge and Oxford. No doubt, Keith-Falconer was caught up in what God was doing during that time.

A portion of a lecture given by Keith-Falconer gives us an idea of the mission zeal of his day:

> Perhaps you try to think that you are meant to remain at home and encourage others to go. You think that by sending money, sitting on committees, speaking at meetings, and praying for missions, you will be doing the most you can to spread the Gospel abroad. Not so! By going yourself you will produce a tenfold more powerful effect. You can give and pray for missions wherever you are. You can send descriptive letters to the missionary meetings which will be more effective than second-hand quotes gathered from others. We have a great and impressive war-office, but a very small army. You have your money invested. You are strong and healthy. You are free to live where you like, and do whatever you want. While vast continents are shrouded in utter darkness, and hundreds and millions are dying without knowing Christ, the burden of proof lies upon you to show that the circumstances in which God has placed you were meant by Him to keep you out of the mission field. (Robson 1922:111-112)

With his heart already stirred by the missionary zeal of his time, and his will already surrendered to wherever God would lead, Keith-Falconer was now ready to hear from God about a specific direction. Sometimes there is much confusion about God's will. We are not sure what we should do or where we should go. However, God has promised to make Himself known to us. He has promised to show us what is His "good, pleasing, and perfect will." We must first surrender ourselves to God. We must first say, "yes," before we know where, when, and what. About the same time that C.T. Studd left for China, Keith-Falconer read an article in *The Christian* written by a Major General Haig. Haig, in his article, called for the evangelization of Arabia. Keith-Falconer was so moved by the article that he immediately asked for an interview with the general.

The general advised that a work should be started in Aden, the southern tip of Arabia. It was an ideal place because it was under the British government, and was an important center on the trade routes to the East. Furthermore, it was a center where caravans converged from many parts of Arabia; thus in Aden, one could minister to Jews, Indians, Somalis, Persians, and many different classes of Arabs. Most importantly, it was a pioneer mission field. Keith-Falconer, like the apostle Paul, wanted to "preach the gospel where Christ was not known."

Keith-Falconer and his wife sailed from London in October 1885. They traveled across the Mediterranean Sea, through the newly opened Suez Canal, and down through the Red Sea. Their journey took three weeks. This first trip was a survey. The people of Aden were very receptive. Keith-Falconer was able to share the gospel boldly and openly. The Arabians were amazed that he already knew Arabic. Keith-Falconer felt strongly that work among the children and medical work would be the best. It seemed to him "almost impossible to work with Muslim adults." After spending six months there, it was decided that the mission would be located at Sheikh Othman, which had a population of 6,000.

Keith-Falconer and his wife spent some time back in London and then sailed back to Sheikh Othman in late 1887. They found a small hut to live in, built a 4-meter by 5-meter "hospital," and began the work. Some trips were taken outside of the protected British areas to do medical work and distribute portions of Scripture. On one of these trips, a Sultan, an Islamic ruler, gladly received Keith-Falconer and his partner, Dr. Cowen. By simply being a friend to Muslims in need, the fame of the mission began to spread into the interior. However, it was not to be that Keith-Falconer would get to see the expansion of the southern Arabian mission. Repeated bouts of malaria finally took his life on May 11, 1888. The hospital eventually developed into a three-storey building, treating hundreds and thousands in the name of Jesus Christ.

Since Ion Keith-Falconer's time, the world has changed both geographically, politically, and technologically. Mission organizations have changed the way they train and send out their missionaries to Muslim countries. Missionaries today spend more time learning the culture and ways of the people in order to preach the gospel in a context in which it will be understood. Some parts of Keith-Falconer's story were not included, but his methods, terminology, and attitude reflected the time in which he lived. For example, many missionaries of the 19th century felt it was their duty to "civilize" while they evangelized. Islam has also changed radically since the Keith-Falconer's time. In the late 19th century, seven-eighths of the Islamic world was under British control. Muslims were a poor, conquered people. Now, because of independence, the discovery of oil and numerical growth, Muslims have worldwide influence.

With all of these changes and the advantage of being able to look back over 100 years of mission history, it is sometimes easy to become critical of these early missionaries and their methods, and in being critical, we miss the point; Ion Keith-Falconer was a friend to Muslims when most did not care. His life was short, but it was full. It was said after his death, "Very visibly he gave to the cause of the Kingdom of our Lord Jesus all he had. His university distinction, his oriental learning, his position in society, his wealth, the bright morning of his married life, and his physical strength. He gave the utmost to the Highest, and he did it gladly." (Robson 1922:78)

6

Samuel M. Zwemer (1867-1952): The Apostle to Islam

"Go and make disciples of all nations" (Mt. 28:19). This command is clear. Straightforward. Jesus did not talk about obstacles. There were no "If it is possible," or "If you have money," or "If you are invited," or "If you have education," or "If it is easy." Jesus' disciples believed these words, and preached the gospel where Christ was not known.

At the end of the 19th century a group of young men were challenged by this verse and a call that "All should go and go to all." Among them were Robert Speer, John R. Mott, and Samuel Zwemer. Zwemer was one of the first 1,000 who signed a commitment card to attempt "The evangelization of the world in this generation." This movement, known as the Student Volunteer Movement, was the greatest mission movement in the history of the Church. The miracle of this student movement is that they almost succeeded in obeying the Great Commission. Through these thousands of young people, the Church was established all over the world.

Since Raymund Lull's effort in the 13th century, there had not been much outreach to Muslims. However, this student movement began to change the attitude of Christians toward the sons of Ishmael. Zwemer, more than any other man in church history, called the Church to go to the most difficult and unrewarding field of all: the Muslim world.

In 50 years of ministry, Zwemer lived in Arabia and Egypt. He traveled the length and breadth of the Islamic world coordinating and training individuals and mission organizations in Muslim ministry. He founded a mission, wrote almost 50 books and hundreds of articles. He taught at Princeton University (a very famous college in America). He was an Arabic scholar and a dynamic preacher. He has been rightly called the "Apostle to Islam."

Samuel Zwemer was born near Holland, Michigan, in 1867. He was the 13th of 15 children. His ancestors had come to America from the country of Holland. They were pioneers. The Dutch were known to be conservative Christians, hard workers, and lovers of education. It is said "almost before they had a roof over their heads they would begin to build their church." (Wilson 1952:25) Zwemer had learned to read Dutch and English by the time he was five years old. Later, in school, he learned to read German. This ability to learn languages would help him in his later life. Growing up, Samuel did not play sports, but enjoyed carpentry and reading books.

Zwemer's father was a pastor and it seemed natural for Samuel that he, too, should enter Christian service. In fact, four of Zwemer's five brothers entered the ministry while one sister spent 40 years as a missionary in China. Late in life, Zwemer spoke of the godly influence of his father saying, "I understood the loving fatherhood of God as Jesus taught it because of what I saw in my own father." (Wilson 1952:22)

Zwemer attended Hope College and worked during vacations to help pay for his school. Some of his jobs included harvesting wheat and selling books. It was during college that Samuel became sure of his calling into Christian service. In the summer of 1886, 250 students met with the famous preacher, D.L. Moody. For one month they studied the Bible, listened to different speakers, and talked to God. At the end of this conference in Mount Hermon, Massachusetts, 100 young people signed a card that said, "I purpose, God willing, to become a foreign missionary." From this meeting several students began a tour of college campuses to make this challenge nationwide. Robert Wilder, one of the original 100, came to Hope College. It was under his dynamic preaching, that Samuel and five of his classmates volunteered for foreign missionary service. Late in life, Zwemer reflected on this one decision. He said, "I am now in my 81st year and have spent 60 years thinking of the Muslim world and its problems. It all began when I signed a card in 1886 expressing the purpose to become a foreign missionary. Little did I realize the way God would lead me across the world of Islam, and guide my pen to call out others. Never have I regretted choosing a hard field or an impossible task." (Wilson 1952:240) That same year Samuel's mother died. Before her death, she told Zwemer "he had been placed in the cradle with the prayer that he might be a missionary." (Wilson 1952:28)

Arabia is the homeland of Islam. This religion is the chief rival of Christianity. Here you will find the most zealous followers of Islam, face the most prospect of persecution with little results, and endure an impossible climate. After seminary studies and medical training, Zwemer and a friend, James Cantine, offered themselves to the Reformed Board (the sending agency of their denomination) to serve in the Arab world; but they were turned down. They were told that such a mission would be foolish and "impractical." Determined, the young enthusiastic pair formed their own mission, the American Arabian Mission. The prayer of Abraham, "Oh that Ishmael might live before thee," was adopted as the motto of the Mission. They immediately began raising support. Zwemer and Cantine traveled approximately 10,000 kilometers that year visiting churches. Their method of raising money was unique. Instead of asking for funds for themselves, Zwemer asked for Cantine's support and Cantine asked for Zwemer's.

In 1889, Cantine sailed for Arabia and Zwemer followed in 1890. Their first task, like all new missionaries was language learning. Arabic, the so-called "language of the angels," is known for its beauty for those who know it, and for its difficulty for those who try to learn it. Zwemer jokingly wrote, "Some of its sounds were borrowed from the camel when it complained of overload." Their second task was to establish a place to begin work. Only one mission had worked in Arabia (the mission founded by Ion Keith-Falconer). There was nearly

2,000 kilometers of coastline along Southern Arabia. The British government did not protect most places in the interior. For over a year, surveys, which were more like adventures, were conducted. Dozens of towns and cities were visited and scripture tracts were sold and distributed. Zwemer writes of his visit to Basrah, which became their first mission station:

> When I came on shore from the boat in December, the English government postmaster welcomed me and showed me much kindness. I was able to rent upper rooms in a house adjoining a mosque and could freely receive visitors. The Arabs received me with less prejudice than I expected. Great numbers came for medical treatment every day. Of the sixty portions of the Word of God that I took with me, forty four were sold before I left. Those who have never seen the word of God, now buy and read it. (Wilson 1952:54)

Samuel changed his name to Dhaif Allah, meaning "guest of God," and with the mission barely established, set out for the interior of Iraq. After several weeks of travel he said, "Twelve hundred kilometers of touring along populated rivers. Twelve hundred kilometers of Muslim empire waiting for the gospel of Jesus Christ. One missionary in Baghdad and two in Basrah; what are these among so many?" (Wilson 1952:58) Another one of his journeys during this time between 1891 and 1895 was to the closed city of Sana'a in Yemen. One event that Zwemer never forgot from this trip was his meeting an old sheikh. Zwemer says, "He kissed the book that was handed to him when he found out it was the

Injil or New Testament." (Wilson 1952:60) As testimony to the sacrifice of these young adventuresome missionaries, Lowell Thomas wrote in the introduction of the book *The Golden Milestone*:

> The names of great explorers are usually written across the pages of history. Not so with the missionary. But in the region where he spends his life, the great missionary is often a legendary figure, and frequently exploration is his sideline. Among the names now a legend along the coast of Arabia are the two Americans who are the authors of this book. The names of Zwemer and Cantine are now a part of the Arabian legend. Today along the whole Persian Gulf coast the sheiks of Arabia still talk of these two pioneer missionaries who had the courage to tell the story of Christianity to the fanatical Muslims. (Wilson 1952:49)

In 1895, after five lonely years as a single missionary, Zwemer fell in love with Amy Wilkes, a missionary nurse from Australia. She was assigned to Baghdad, Iraq. In those days, mission boards had strict rules about young lady missionaries having gentlemen friends visit them. However, Zwemer was never lacking in plans. After a friendship through correspondence, he went to Baghdad where he taught Arabic to the young ladies. Their love grew for each other (they must not have been studying language all the time!) and they were married in Baghdad in May 1896.

After sailing to the United States for furlough in 1897, the Zwemers returned to the Persian Gulf to work among the

Muslims on the Island of Basrah. They handed out literature and conducted evangelism in public as well as in private homes, but rarely did they witness any positive results. Living conditions were very hard. Before the days of air conditioning, the heat was almost unbearable, sometimes being 107 degrees Fahrenheit in the shade. Personal tragedy also interfered with the work. In July of 1904, the Zwemers' two little daughters, ages four and seven, both died within a week of each other. They buried their daughters and wrote on their tombstones, "Worthy is the Lamb to receive riches." Despite the persecution, pain, and hardship, the Zwemers continued to serve the Lord. He had "learned the secret of being content in every circumstance." Zwemer could look back on this period some 50 years later and say, "The sheer joy of it all comes back. Gladly would I do it all over again." (Tucker 1983:277)

By 1905, the American Arabia Mission had established four stations, and though there were few in number, the converts showed great courage in their new faith. In that year, the Zwemers returned to the United States. This furlough was the end of their pioneer missionary work among the Muslims. For almost four years, Zwemer traveled across America raising money and mobilizing young people to go and be friends to the Muslim world. Many students answered the call to foreign missions. It is not surprising when you hear some of the testimonies and quotes from these conventions. He spoke with passion and conviction. Robert Speer said, "I have never forgotten the speech of Dr. Zwemer...when he hung a great map of Islam before us, and with a sweep of his hand across all those darkened areas he said, 'You O Christ are all I want; and You O Christ are all they want. What Christ can do for any man, He can do for every man.'" (Wilson 1952:168) In another conference, Zwemer pled for missionaries to go to the Holy Land, then called Western Asia. He said,

> His manger and His cross stood there. In Western Asia His blood was spilled. In Western Asia He walked the hills. There His tears fell for Jerusalem. There He will come again. It was in Western Asia that He said, 'All authority is given unto Me;' Shall we give Western Asia to Him, or shall Western Asia remain the empire of Muhammad? Shall Bethlehem hear five times a day 'There is no god but Allah, and Muhammad is Allah's apostle,' and shall not a single one of us dare go, if God wills, in this year of our Lord nineteen hundred and ten to Mecca itself, the very stronghold of Islam, and preach the Gospel of the great King? (Wilson 1952:170)

In 1910, the Zwemers returned to the Gulf region, but they found it hard to get back into their work. Zwemer's leadership abilities were in great demand. He was often asked to plan conferences and speak in many places. Then, in 1912, he received a call to come to Cairo, Egypt in order to coordinate all Muslim work in the world. In Cairo, Zwemer found a far more open society. Egypt was known as the intellectual center of Islam. Educated young adults were eager to listen to Zwemer. Sometimes as many as 2,000 Muslims attended his lectures! He spent many hours each week visiting campuses. He even gained access to proud and influential Muslim University El Azhar. Zwemer recorded once in a newsletter: "During the past few months I have found many who are responsive. A number of teachers want copies of the Bible...we were able to give nearly a dozen Bibles to professors, and over 150 copies of Matthew's Gospel to students." (Wilson 1952:88)

For 17 years Zwemer made Cairo his headquarters. From there he traveled all over the world holding conferences, raising funds, and helping establish work among Muslims in India, China, Indochina, and South Africa. In all of these places he collected data concerning how many Muslims lived in each place and how many missionaries were working among them. It is interesting to note that in 1922 there were 16 Protestant missions at work in Java, with a total of 456 missionaries in all the islands of Indonesia. Today there are around 3,000 missionaries. However, in spite of this large number, Indonesia still contains 130 people groups larger than 10,000 people, which have a Christian population of less than 1%. Zwemer reported that at the time of his visit, there were 210,000 Batak Christians in Sumatra, where Samuel Munson and Henry Lyman were martyred in 1834. He visited their grave and found this inscription written:

Here Rest the Bones
of the two American Missionaries
Munson and Lyman
Killed and eaten in the year, 1834.
John 16:1-3
*"The blood of the Martyrs is the seed of the church of
Jesus"*
(Wilson 1952:124)

God is still at work among this people group. Batak Christians now number around four million! Some are beginning to be friends with the sons of Ishmael, but many more friends are needed.

In 1924, after touring Iran, Zwemer found 162 missionaries serving there. He said, "Iran is a difficult field, one that appeals to the heroic and that test men's souls, but it is a place white unto harvest." (Wilson 1952:130) Today, missionaries are not allowed to minister in Iran. The Bible Society, all Christian bookstores, conferences, camps, printing of literature, and production of videos are banned, but despite fierce persecution, forced church closures, imprisonment and murder of pastors, the body of Christ inside of Iran is growing. It has also been noted by the Iranian Christians International Inc. that there are 20,000 Evangelical Iranian Christians living outside Iran." (www.farsinet.com/ici/who.html) Also, on this survey, Zwemer called for the evangelization of Afghanistan, but this call fell on deaf ears. This country is still one of the least reached countries in the world.

After his tour of India, he commented on the church planting movement that had taken place in Medak, but said that even though India had over 5,000 missionaries "Muslim India is an unoccupied field." (Wilson 1952:143) The results of Zwemer's survey of China in 1933 were published in an Atlas for Missions, giving the approximate number of Muslims in each province of China. The purpose of these surveys was to call out a sleeping Church! After 70 years, the call continues! The Church is still sleeping, while these lands and peoples have few friends. They are still unoccupied lands! The answer is not more knowledge or surveys, but a "new man" as Zwemer preached. He said, "A study of the lives of great men who opened various countries to the gospel, reveal that they possess several qualities sometimes absent from the modern missionary: vision, knowledge (of the language and the people), persistence, passion for souls and the ability to endure loneliness. It is a new man rather than a new method that is needed." (Wilson 1952:160)

In 1929, with his work well established, Zwemer accepted an invitation to become a professor at Princeton University. He had been a missionary for 40 years. He called his move to Princeton "The Third Milestone." The first milestone had been his pioneering work in Arabia, the second was his time in Cairo, and the third was Princeton Seminary. Besides his teaching, the remainder of Zwemer's life was filled with speaking and writing. Even when he turned 70, he gave a speech entitled "Life Begins At Seventy." To the very end, he was filled with a "nervous energy" and continual mental activity. One traveling companion once recounted his overnight stay with Zwemer: "He could not stay in bed for more than 30 minutes at a time... for then, on would go the light, Zwemer would get out of bed, get some paper and pencil, write a few sentences and then again to bed." (Tucker 1983:279) It is no wonder that he accomplished so much in his life. One man commented that Zwemer did more in his life than most of us could do if we lived as long as Methuselah.

After his death at the age of 84 his grandson wrote,

> It is very sad to think that we have lost a wonderful grandfather and that the world has lost a wonderful preacher. His sermons were well written and well read, but they really came alive when he was up in the pulpit pounding with one hand, while holding a train schedule in his other hand...I am afraid that Grandfather will stir up too much activity until he finds out that Heaven is a place of rest. (Wilson 1952:246)

Samuel Zwemer, in his life, travels, books, sermons, articles, conversations, and prayers reveals to us a man totally committed to making friends with the sons of Ishmael. Zwemer's favorite hymn was: "Christian, do you see them?" Well, do you?

Section 3

7

Franklin Graham (1952-   ):
A Modern Day
Good Samaritan

It was a cold, rainy January afternoon when the plane landed in Cyprus. I headed straight for the dock where I boarded an old cargo ship. It was now well after dark. The boat was old and rusty. The plan called for me to meet a small dinghy, several miles off the coast of Lebanon, and then sneak into the country. The old boat I was riding, slowly made its way across the Mediterranean Sea. As the Lebanon shore came into view, I looked across the rough waters of the Sea, wondering if I had made a bad decision. The country was at war! The small boat met us several miles off the coast, so we would be out of artillery range of the Syrian army. The giant waves kept slamming the little boat against the rusted hull of our boat. The waves would push the boats apart and then back together making the transfer more of a challenge than I had expected.

I would have to jump from the big vessel to the small boat, timing it perfectly. If I missed, I might not have another chance to try. I would find myself, either swimming in the cold, black waters of the Mediterranean or smashed between the two hulls of the boats as they crashed together. Studying the rough sea, I took a deep breath and threw myself over the edge of the ship across the cold water. With a satisfying thud, I felt my feet hit the deck of the small boat. (Graham 1998:55-57)

No, this story is not a script from the latest adventure movie, nor is it a classified, government document of the C.I.A. or Special Ops mission. This story is one of the many adventures of Franklin Graham, CEO of Samaritan's Purse, an international Christian relief organization. The year was 1982. Franklin Graham was risking his life to bring relief and help to Palestinians in the refugee camps of Sabra and Shatila.

Bob Pierce founded Samaritan's Purse in 1970. After World War II, Pierce traveled in many different parts of the world with a ministry called Youth for Christ. It was on these trips that he saw ordinary people trying to help others who had both physical and spiritual needs. Pierce wrote these words in his Bible, "Let my heart be broken with the things that break the heart of God." This passionate prayer, the needs of the world, and the story of the Good Samaritan is what guided Pierce to found Samaritan's Purse. Franklin Graham did not become the leader of Samaritan's Purse until 1978, after Bob Pierce died of leukemia. The organization has grown from two full-time employees to over 400, having worldwide impact.

To understand Franklin Graham and the ministry of Samaritan's Purse, let us look again at one of the greatest stories in the Bible: the Good Samaritan.

> But he wanted to justify himself, so he asked Jesus, "And who is my neighbor?" In reply Jesus said: "A man was going down from Jerusalem to Jericho, when he fell into the hands of robbers. They stripped him of his clothes, beat him and went away, leaving him half dead. A priest happened to be going down the same road and when he saw the man, he passed by on the other side. So too, a Levite, when he came to the place and saw him, passed by on the other side. But a Samaritan, as he traveled, came where the man was; and when he saw him, he took pity on him. He went to him and bandaged his wounds, pouring on oil and wine. Then he put the man on his own donkey, took him to an inn and took care of him. The next day he took out two silver coins and gave them to the innkeeper. 'Look after him,' he said, 'and when I return, I will reimburse you for any extra expense you may have.' Which of these three do you think was a neighbor to the man who fell into the hands of robbers?" The expert in the law replied, "The one who had mercy on him." Jesus told him, "Go and do likewise" (Luke 10:30-37).

In this story are several truths that help Graham's ministry stay focused. One is that the Samaritan in the parable was probably a layperson. He was ordinary. He was not a professional minister. Samaritan's Purse is an organization of ordinary people doing extraordinary things. Second, when the Samaritan saw the victim of robbery, he was moved with compassion. Something happened down deep in his heart. Even though this dying man was his racial enemy, the Samaritan showed kindness and mercy. He went to him. Samaritan's Purse, because of compassion, makes the effort to go where the needs are the greatest. It does not matter who, what religion, or how far. Samaritan's Purse is committed to go and help in the name of Jesus. Third, the Samaritan bandaged up the victim's wounds, put him on his donkey, took him to a hotel, and paid the bill. The Samaritan provided shelter, medicine, food, and clothing. He did for the man what he could not do for himself. The Samaritan sacrificed his time and money until the victim was able to recover. It was a one-time-stepping-in-to-meet-a-critical-need kind of help. The man could never repay the Samaritan, and the Samaritan did not expect anything for his kindness. Bob Pierce often spoke of this third principle as "our reason for being." Fourth, because of his act of unselfish love, the Samaritan had earned the right to be heard. Graham's relief ministry is unashamedly bold in sharing the gospel of Jesus Christ. It does not matter whether they are doing relief in a Buddhist, Hindu, or Muslim country. The gospel is presented. Graham says that many times their team is asked, "Why have you come to help us?" Graham's answer is always the same: "We have come to help you in the name of the Lord Jesus Christ." Because of this boldness to share the good news of Jesus Christ, there are some who might question or oppose this approach of ministry. Some accuse relief or development ministries of taking advantage of people or offering help as "bait." However, Harold Watson, a well-known agriculturalist and community developer in Southeast

Asia says, "We do not use our farming technology or relief as bait. We help the poor, because Jesus said, 'Love your neighbor as yourself.'"

Samaritan's Purse, as an organization, knows that having an earthly shelter without a heavenly home is not enough. They know that giving medicine for the body without healing the soul is spiritual malpractice. Graham believes that giving food to the hungry and water to the thirsty without telling about the true Bread of Life and the Living Water is not really keeping the vision of being a true neighbor.

This vision to be a true neighbor has led Graham and Samaritan's Purse to go behind enemy lines in Nicaragua in the late 1980s, dodge bullets in Beirut, Lebanon, and bring hope to the Tutsi minority of Rwanda in 1994. The Hutu majority blamed the Tutsi tribe for the death of their president, who was a Hutu. In a matter of three months the Hutu killed an estimated 1,500,000 Tutsi people.

In 2004, Samaritan's Purse went to the refugee camps of Darfur, Sudan. In the past two years, over 300,000 people in Darfur have died of violence, disease, and malnutrition. Samaritan's Purse was able to feed more than 100,000 Sudanese during 2004, thus, saving them from death. When hurricane Ivan devastated the tiny island nation of Grenada, Samaritan's Purse responded by providing emergency relief supplies and temporary housing for 250 families. Graham helped war refugees in northern Uganda, a village of outcasts in southern Cambodia, AIDS victims in Africa, and gave 7.4 million Christmas gifts to children all over the world.

Graham has proven to be a modern day "Good Samaritan," by being a true friend and neighbor to Muslims worldwide. Franklin Graham may be the 21st century's greatest friend to Ishmael. He said, "I have lived in the Middle East. I have a great love for the Arab people and for those of the Islamic faith. After all, they are of the seed of Abraham." (Graham 1995:235) Two-thirds of all refugees are Muslims. Eighty percent of the poorest people on earth are Muslims. Some of the greatest tragedies of history in 2004 and 2005 happened in Islamic countries. Where Muslims are hurting and in need, Graham has responded.

When the tsunami hit Asia in December 2004, Samaritan's Purse went to help. Christians are providing permanent housing for 3,000 families in Indonesia. The first of these housing projects was completed in July 2005. Government officials came together with Samaritan's Purse personnel to dedicate the first 50 new concrete houses. Indonesian officials said this is the first project of its kind; rebuilding permanent homes for an entire community. Samaritan's Purse set up a water treatment plant to meet the daily needs of 15,000 people in Kalmunai, Sri Lanka. Twenty-five thousand mosquito nets were taken to remote villages in Indonesia, and over 2,800 wells have been cleaned and repaired. Doctors and nurses have been transported by helicopter to remote areas, and have treated or vaccinated over 14,000 people for measles and malaria. Hundreds of fishing boats and equipment have been provided. Graham and other Christian organizations have continued to work in the affected areas of the tsunami, even after others have packed up and gone home. One relief worker in Asia quoted a local Muslim official saying, "Christians are the only ones who have come to help us."

In October 2005, an earthquake registering 7.8 on the Richter scale hit the mountainous regions of Pakistan and India. Eighty thousand people were killed and three million were left homeless. The cries of the victims were heard loud and clear. CNN reporters reported the plight of these special people into our living rooms. Most of us turned the channel, thinking there was not much we could do. However, within two weeks, Graham had sent a 747 airplane packed with rolls of plastic to shelter up to 20,000 people. Also included in the shipment were 10,000 blankets, 350 wheelchairs, and other urgently needed supplies. Efforts are still going on because Graham is a true friend to Muslims. He is a modern day Good Samaritan.

Franklin Graham was not always the "Good Samaritan." In fact, there was a time, when he was not good at all. He was a "prodigal son" (Lk. 15:11-32). He was rebellious against his parents and against God. Franklin's father is the famous evangelist, Billy Graham. Dr. Graham has preached to more people than any man in history (over 100,000,000). He has conducted crusades in over 185 countries. Dr. Graham has been a friend and spiritual adviser to eight United States presidents. He has had the privilege to meet and talk with kings, queens, politicians, scholars, popes, bishops, dictators, and movie stars. Dr. Graham has been "knighted" by England (the highest honor), and has received the Congressional Gold Medal from the United States government (the highest honor the Congress of the United States can bestow on a citizen).

Franklin was born (1952) and raised in the mountains of North Carolina. In his own words, he is a country boy. He has always loved camping, hunting, and anything with a loud motor. Like many small boys growing up in the 1950s in America, Franklin had a complete set of cowboy gear: boots, jeans, shirt, hat and most importantly, a holster and a toy pistol. He spent many hours playing in the nearby woods chasing imaginary robbers and shooting animals with his "pistol."

Franklin's daddy was often away from home for weeks and months preaching in crusades. Franklin knew that his daddy was off doing something very important, but he did not fully understand. He only knew that when his daddy was away he really missed him. Franklin also admits that when he was young, he had a strong will. He says, "When I wanted to do something, I did it even if I knew I would be disobeying my parents and risking punishment." (Franklin 1995:10) Franklin's strong will and absent father led to some comical confrontations between him and his mother, Ruth.

Franklin, at an early age, began to pick up cigarette butts and smoke them. When Ruth could not get him to stop, she forced him to smoke a whole pack of cigarettes, causing Franklin to throw up several times. One time when Franklin would not behave in the car, Ruth pulled over and, after making sure he could breathe, locked Franklin in the trunk of the car for the remainder of the ride.

In spite of Franklin's rebellious nature and many "encounters" with his mother, he grew up in a very loving, supportive Christian home. They went to church every Sunday, learned stories from the

Bible, had family devotions, and memorized Scripture verses. Both Billy and Ruth lived the Christian life inside and outside the home.

When Franklin was 13, he was sent to Stony Brook School for Boys in New York. Franklin recalls his feelings:

> 'I felt a dull ache in my chest. This was the worst nightmare coming true. They weren't punishing me by sending me away, but it felt like it. I was devastated. I knew I would not be happy living anywhere else but the mountains of North Carolina.' He continues, 'Then that moment I had dreaded for so long came, when Daddy had to say good-bye and leave me there alone. I can still remember hugging and kissing him and watching the car disappear. I don't think I have ever had a more lonely feeling than I did at that moment. I ached.' (Franklin 1995:32-34)

Franklin never liked going to school at Stony Brook. Being a Southerner, he was treated like an outsider. He felt like a prisoner. He was slowly becoming more and more rebellious. By his sophomore year in high school, he was smoking all the time and drinking beer whenever he could. By the middle of his junior year, Franklin was about to be expelled from school. He convinced his parents to allow him to come home to Montreat and finish high school.

After high school, Franklin worked for the summer in the state of Alaska. The job was hard and the workdays were long, but Franklin had never had so much "freedom." He spent every night in local bars playing cards and getting drunk.

In Franklin's first year of college, God began to use people and circumstances to cause him to surrender his life to Christ.

Franklin enrolled in LeTourneau College in Texas. One of the first people that Franklin met was Bill Cristobal. Bill had just finished three combat tours as a helicopter pilot in Vietnam. He was mature and focused in life. More importantly, Bill had a strong relationship with Jesus Christ. Bill and Franklin became very good friends. They had a lot in common. They both loved airplanes, loud engines, and the outdoors. They spent many nights camping and talking. One of the things that impressed Franklin about Bill's life is that he was a genuine Christian that "wasn't stuffy or uptight, and he really knew how to have fun."

Another influence on Franklin was Roy Gustafson, and associate with the Billy Graham Evangelistic Association (BGEA). Every summer, Roy led Bible tours through the Middle East. The summer after his freshman year in college, Franklin worked for Roy, handling all of the logistics of the touring groups. Franklin says, "even though he was thirty-seven years older, he soon became one of my best friends." (Franklin 1995:82) Roy was an excellent Bible teacher. Every night, the group would gather to study God's word. For the first time in his life, Franklin began to enjoy the Bible.

Another aspect of the trip was visiting different ministries throughout the Middle East. One ministry they visited was a hospital in Mafraq, Jordan. Franklin did not know it at the time, but this visit would lay the foundation for his life work of helping and supporting front line workers serving in difficult places. Two single ladies, Dr. Eleanor Soltau and Aileen Coleman ran the hospital. "They were gutsy and tough." Their hospital was a spiritual oasis in a very dry place. When Franklin discovered that the hospital needed a new vehicle, he convinced his dad to help purchase a fully loaded Land Rover. Franklin sold his car, and he and Bill Cristobal personally delivered the vehicle to Mafraq, Jordan. Their adventure took them six weeks. They traveled thousands of kilometers, across nine countries.

Franklin and Bill stayed at the hospital for several weeks, mixing cement, making cement blocks, and digging ditches. Franklin was impressed by the faith, love, and commitment he saw in Eleanor and Aileen. Prayers were answered, sometimes in dramatic ways. Money would "arrive right on time, just when they needed it." Also, even though Franklin was still drinking and smoking, never once did the missionaries "preach" to him. They accepted him and loved him.

Finally, God sent David Hill to help bring Franklin, "the Prodigal," back home to Christ. David had a powerful testimony. He had been saved out of the occult, drugs, and the mafia. He had long blond hair, wore stylish clothes, drove a nice car, and carried a .9 mm pistol. Franklin was impressed! David and Franklin spent the summer of 1974 together in Lausanne, Switzerland, helping with logistics of an international congress for evangelism. While there, Franklin celebrated his twenty-second birthday with his parents. Franklin relates,

> After the meal, Daddy and I walked along a pathway beside the lake. My father looked at me and said, 'Franklin, your mother and I sense there is a struggle going on in your life.' His father continued, 'You're going to have to make a choice either to accept Christ or reject Him. You can't continue to play the middle ground. Either you are going to choose to follow and

obey Him or reject Him. I want you to know we are proud of you, Franklin. We love you no matter what you do in life, and no matter where you go. The door of our home is always open, and you are always welcome. But you are going to have to make a choice.' (Franklin 1995:123)

After this conversation, Franklin spent many days thinking about what his father had said. He talked some more with David, read and re-read Romans 7 and 8, and John 3. He realized he was not "in" Christ. His life was empty. Franklin was tired of running from God. He says, "I put my cigarette out and got down on my knees beside my bed. I poured my heart out to God and confessed my sin. I was His. I invited Him by faith to come into my life." (Franklin 1995:123)

Franklin did not become CEO of Samaritan's Purse until he was 28 years old. Therefore, the next six years of Franklin's life were filled with many activities, spiritual markers, and lessons. He married Jane Austin, finished college, and spent a year in Bible college. In October 1975, God began to use Bob Pierce to direct and mentor Franklin. Bob took Franklin on a two-month world tour so that he could show Franklin the poverty of pagan religions and the hopelessness and despair of the people.

While traveling, Bob taught Franklin some truths, which still guide the work of Samaritan's Purse. One of these lessons is what Bob called *"God room."*

God room is 'when you see a need and it is bigger than your human abilities to meet it. But you accept the challenge. You trust God to bring in the finances and the materials to meet the need. You get together with your staff, prayer partners, and supporters, and you pray. Then you begin to watch God work. Before you know it, the need is met. At the same time, you understand you did not do it. God did it. You allowed Him room to work.' Bob continued, 'Faith is not required as long as you set your goal only as high as the most intelligent, most informed, and expert human efforts can reach. Nothing is a miracle until it reaches the area where the utmost that human effort can do still is not enough. God has to fill that space, or room, between what is possible and what He wants done that is impossible. That is what I mean by *God room*.' (Franklin 1995:140)

Another lesson that Bob taught was what he called "having guts for Jesus." Another way to say this would be "being tough for Jesus." Whenever Bob would see some Christian or missionary working in a very difficult place, maybe in the midst of war, or in the middle of jungle, he would say, "they have guts for Jesus." They are the ones that need to be helped and encouraged by ministries such as Samaritan's Purse. They are serving the Lord in the unreached and hard to reach places. The apostle Paul is the greatest example of someone having "guts for Jesus." He was beaten, stoned, whipped, cursed, and hated, but he never stopped preaching the gospel. He said, "I consider my life worth nothing to me if only I may finish the race and complete the task the Lord Jesus has given me; the task of testifying to the gospel of God's grace" (Acts 20:24).

What our world needs are more believers who live by the "God room" principle. What our world needs are more disciples who have "guts for Jesus," who will go to the unreached and hard to reach. What our world needs are more "Good Samaritans," who will be moved with compassion and show love and kindness to those in need, even the sons of Ishmael.

(Adapted from Rebel With A Cause: Finally Comfortable Being Graham; by Franklin Graham, Thomas Nelson, Inc. Nashville, Tenn. 1995)

8

Making Friends Behind the Veil: The Story of Heather Mercer and Dayna Curry

"Mommy, why am I doing this?" Eight-year-old Habiba rubbed her tired eyes. Half asleep and still in her pajamas, she could hardly stand up straight. "We simply have to do it, little one," her mother answered, as she unrolled the prayer rugs. It was barely dawn. "If I am praying, there should be someone listening," Habiba murmured, struggling to stay awake. "He should answer. He should be like Daddy. When I talk to him, he answers. I respect God. I honor him. Why doesn't he talk to me?" At age seven, little Habiba had been veiled. In her very orthodox Muslim home, she prayed five times a day. Her mother was her mentor. (Adeney 2002:44)

Veiled at seven. Mentored by parents. Isolated by culture. Pressured by family and at times suppressed by Islamic law. Who will reach the daughters of Hagar? Where are the young

Christian ladies who will give up all to make friends with those living behind the veil? Where are the pioneers like Mildred Cable, who in the early 20th century crossed the Gobi Desert five times preaching the gospel? Her book, *The Gobi Desert*, describes how she and her friends risked their lives to make friends with Chinese Muslims behind the Great Wall of China.

Almost one-tenth of the world's population is Muslim women. Reaching these women may be the greatest challenge to the Church today. One Christian worker expressed her frustration this way,

> In Tashkent, I first saw women fully covered in Islamic dress. I would see the women walking in groups on the city's main square, and I would want to talk to them. They wore black coverings called *chadors*. I could see the women's eyes through the slits in the fabric. I remember thinking, how do you approach such a woman? How do you offer her love and comfort? How can you reach her? (Curry 2002:37)

The veil, which was never commanded by Muhammad, is a complex issue within Islam. Not all Muslims agree and different Islamic countries require different degrees of covering. To the uninformed follower of Jesus, the veil can give many false messages about the Muslim woman such as: *We Muslims are all the same...I am not interested in the gospel...I do not want to be your friend...We have nothing in common...I am a terrorist...I am a committed Muslim...I know much about Islam*. Miriam Adeney lists five other myths about Muslim women.

1. Muslim women are passive and submissive. They rarely think for themselves or exert much leadership.
2. Muslim women usually cannot come to Christ and grow in Christ unless their husbands become believers, too.
3. A Muslim family will feel more threatened if a daughter or wife believes in Christ as Lord than if a son or husband does.
4. Muslim women and men can be evangelized and discipled together effectively, using the same strategies and the same Scripture texts.
5. Muslim women should not be evangelized until there is a Christian man available to evangelize the men, since women will not lead to a lasting fellowship.

Every Muslim woman is different. They have been created in the image of God with unique gifts and personalities. Their nationality, language, culture, and family make them different. There are Arab women. East of Arabia, we find Iranian Muslim women, who are different both religiously and culturally. Muslims speaking Turkish languages number over one hundred million. Most of these live in the former Soviet Union. Muslims populate much of North Africa and South Asia. Indonesia has the largest Muslim population of any country in the world. As different as these nations are from each other, so are the Muslim women different who live in these countries. A woman's concerns will also be shaped by

- Her age
- Her economic situation
- Her personality

- Whether she is single
- Whether she is a married mother
- Whether she is a childless married woman
- Whether she is a divorced mother
- Whether she is a student in the West

Most Arab village women raise children and work at home. In Cairo, Egypt, many women work outside the home. In the Middle East, Muslim women are professionals. For example, in Tunisia, 25% of the judges are women, as are 20% in Morocco. In Saudi Arabia, working women are estimated to be slightly more than 250,000. Women-only shopping malls, gymnasiums, business centers, and Internet cafes are a new trend in places like Saudi Arabia, Pakistan, and Abu Dhabi. Muslim women are not the same, and because of these differences, no one strategy will work. However, God has made every human heart the same. The human heart is empty until Christ lives there.

Worldwide, Muslim women are interested in spiritual things. They are asking questions. On campuses in the West, they are looking for a friend. Behind their veils, many Muslim women are searching for truth, forgiveness, hope, and purpose, because they have not found these things in Islam. Simin, an Iranian woman, searched for God for years. When she came to America, it took several months before she met a true believer. In frustration she prayed, "God, I've been looking for You everywhere and I can't find You. Why

You hiding? You are cruel! Can't You hear somebody calling for You?"

We do not need anymore strategies nor do we need anymore prayer walking teams to go for a week, pray, then go home, thinking the Great Commission has been obeyed. The call is for thousands of young ladies who will allow the gospel to interrupt their lives, plans, ambitions and go and live among these Muslim women.

God is calling this generation to follow the example of Dayna Curry and Heather Mercer who, in 2001, dared to take the gospel into Afghanistan. For over 20 years this country had been at war. For over a decade the Soviet Union fought US-backed Islamic rebels. After the Soviets withdrew in 1989, civil war followed between different tribes. The country's cities and infrastructure were destroyed. In 1994, the Taliban, which means "religious students," came to power with the help of Pakistan and Osama bin Laden's well-financed Al Qaeda organization. They enforced strict Islamic law or *shariat*, and brought some order to the country. However, the "order" they brought was like trading one evil for another. Public beatings and executions were common. Music, television, photography, and movies were outlawed. Men were required to wear full beards and there were many restrictions for women. The women were required to wear *burqus*, which are shiny garments that fit over the head and cover the body with mesh screens for the eyes. Women were not permitted to work and girls were not allowed to attend school. Women were allowed to ride buses, but they were required to sit in a curtained-off area in the back. A woman professor who fled Afghanistan in the mid-1990s said, "We hate the Taliban; they are against all civilization, Afghan culture, education, and women in particular. They have given Islam and the Afghan people a bad name. The children of the Taliban are growing up with no education and only a knowledge of guns and opium." (Adeney 2002:31)

Even before the terrorist attack on America in 2001, the Taliban was known to be training terrorists and protecting Osama bin Laden. In fact, only Pakistan, Saudi Arabia, and the United Arab Emirates recognized the Taliban as a true government. Humanly speaking, Afghanistan under the Taliban was an impossible place to go and preach the gospel. What is it that led Dayna and Heather to go to this country? What could they possibly do there?

Dayna Curry says, "I desired to extend friendship to veiled women long before I ever went to Afghanistan—perhaps because I had known isolation myself." (Curry 2002:30) Dayna's isolation came because of her sinful life. As a teenager, she lived far away from God. She experimented with drugs and drank alcoholic beverages. At the age of 16, she became sexually involved with her boyfriend. She became pregnant on her seventeenth birthday and a few weeks later had an abortion. She recalled, "After the abortion, I felt like a stone. I felt dead inside." (Curry 2002:33) During her fourth year of high school, Dayna began to know that God was drawing her to Himself. However, she did not give her life to Christ until her first year in college. It was there she met a group of young people who were in her words, "alive, loving, and passionate for God." Dayna says that the night she accepted Christ it was as if "waves of heat were washing over me. I knew God was touching me. For the first time I knew I was forgiven." "For those who have been forgiven much, love much," said Jesus. This verse explained Dayna's new life in Christ. Christ had changed her life. She began to love Jesus with all her heart and the natural result of that love was giving her life in service to others. While still in college, Dayna participated in several short-term mission trips to other countries. These trips helped prepare her for the future and helped her understand what God was calling her to do. One of her favorite verses was Isaiah's words, "Here am I, send me."

Heather Mercer's testimony is not as dramatic as Dayna's, but just as real. She says, "As a high school student, I was driven and purposeful. Even at a young age, I wanted to be successful and make a difference in society. To others, I seemed to have my life together, but I struggled with insecurity, fear of failure, and fear of rejection. I wondered where I fit. What was my place in the world." (Curry 2002:16) When she was a teenager, her parents divorced, causing her much pain. She began to search for true love.

One night, with some friends, she attended a concert at a church. The speaker explained that Jesus' love was not dependent on what people did. He explained that this love was free, and that Jesus could heal broken bodies and hearts. Heather explains,

> The love of other people had left me feeling empty.
> I wanted something lasting and life-changing, something

real. The message of love spoke to my heart. That evening, as the speaker prayed aloud, I prayed along with him. I asked Jesus to give me His love and heal my broken heart. I told Jesus I would follow Him if He would show me where to go. (Curry 2002:18)

When Heather went to Baylor University, she began to attend the same church where Dayna was a member. This church had fervent worship and a desire to demonstrate God's love to all nations. Heather states,

Through my church's teaching, I started to learn more about people from other cultures and nations. Poverty, disease, and famines plagued several of the countries we studied. As I read the Bible, one particular passage caught my attention.... "He defended the cause of the poor and needy...is this not what it means to know me?" declares the LORD (Jer. 22:26). I came to realize that my love for God would be directly expressed through my service to the poor. I had been blessed with so much in life; I had a responsibility to give myself to those with less. (Curry 2002:19)

One Scripture that spoke to Heather was, "And from everyone who has been given much shall much be required" (Lk. 12:48 NASB).

We come back to the question I asked earlier. What is it that led Dayna and Heather to go to Afghanistan?

1. They both had experienced God's love through a personal relationship with Jesus Christ.

2. They both were involved in a church that was alive with worship and involved in missions.
3. They both were involved in local ministries and short-term missions.
4. They both were challenged by the Word of God to obey the Great Commission.
5. They both were involved in a church that was actively ministering to and offering opportunities in the country of Afghanistan. In other words, the opportunity was there.
6. They both began to pray and seek the Lord for guidance.
7. They both were willing to go to the unreached and hard to reach.

Let's listen to Dayna and Heather as they made their decision to go. Heather says, "As my vision about sharing God's love with the poor in other countries, I began to pray this way, 'Lord, send me to the hardest place. Send me where others do not want to go or are afraid to go.'" (Curry 2002:20) Dayna states, "After much prayerful consideration, I believed God simply was looking for someone who was willing to go wherever there might be a need." (Curry 2002:36) Dayna continues, "Whether you feel called and go, or volunteer and go, the end result is the same; your fulfillment and reward will be the same. I did not need some big dramatic calling or vision to go to Afghanistan. I could just go. It actually seemed crazy not to go, since so few people were willing to serve in such a desolate place." (Curry 2002:38)

Afghanistan in the late 1990s was a third world, war-ravaged, drought-stricken country, having a military government, and serving as the training ground for an international terrorist organization with America as its number one enemy. As can be expected, family and friends had many concerns and objections to Dayna and Heather going to Afghanistan. They were asked, "Aren't you being foolish?" "Why would you risk your own safety?" Similar questions are posed to us as we send teams of young people into potentially dangerous places. Parents write and want us to "assure the safety of their children." Students also search the Internet, filling their mind with bad news and then have doubts about coming and serving. Some people listen to the U.S. embassy's warnings about personal safety more than Jesus' warnings of eternal punishment for those without Christ.

Dayna and Heather have a great response to the issue of "safety."

> Many individuals choose to put themselves in harm's way every day because they believe in what they are doing: police officers, firefighters, journalists, U.S. Special Forces, United Nations peacekeepers. These people sacrifice their own security to pursue their passions, convictions, and dreams. We were no different. Our dream was to go to the hard-to-reach places and demonstrate God's love by serving the poorest of the poor. (Curry 2002:40)

Knowing that witnessing was prohibited and conversion was punishable by death, they wanted simply to be able to look even one poor widow in the eye and tell her of God's love. When they boarded the plane and finally drove through mountains leading to the capital city of Kabul, they could never have dreamed what God had planned for them nor how He would use them.

Dayna and Heather worked with Shelter Germany, a non-profit organization that was involved in building houses, relief work, and community development. However, much of their time was spent talking to and helping widows and street children. They had not come to "convert" the Afghan people. That is something only God can do. They had come to love them and serve them in the name of Jesus. Many asked them why they had come. They boldly responded, "Because God totally changed our lives and healed our broken hearts with His love. He also loves you and has a purpose for your life." (Curry 2002:42)

In this "closed" country, many Afghans asked Dayna and Heather about Jesus. They said the topic of religion came up every day. They testified that in this "hard-to-reach" place, they talked about Jesus continually because the people would not stop asking them about their God!

When they prayed with or for people, they always asked permission to pray in the name of Jesus. Permission was always granted. Sometimes miraculous healings took place in the name of Jesus. The two young ladies, in a natural way, shared Christ's love with their friends in private settings. Ultimately, this "trying to convert Muslims to Christianity" led to their arrest and imprisonment for three months. While in prison, they ministered to Afghan women, testified faithfully about Christ to Taliban officials, and endured the daily bombing raids of the US-led invasion of Afghanistan. Sometimes the bombs were so close that their whole prison shook and windows were blown out. Finally, Dayna and Heather, along with six other aid workers were rescued by U.S. Special Forces.

The complete story of Dayna Curry and Heather Mercer, as told *in Prisoners of Hope*, is like an adventure movie, complete with a happy ending. It is a story of changed lives and simple obedience to God's Word. It is a story of ordinary young ladies picking up their crosses and going to the unreached and hard-to-reach. But more than that, this is a story of God's love for a desperate and oppressed people. It is a story of God searching for the lost and hurting of Afghanistan. "Surely the arm of the LORD is not too short to save, nor his ear too dull to hear" (Isa. 59:1). This story reminds us that there are really no "closed" countries nor unreachable people. Brother Andrew, who heads a ministry called Open Doors, said:

> There is not a door in the world closed where you want to witness for Jesus...Show me a closed door and I will tell you how to get in. I will not however, promise you a way to get out. Jesus did not say, "Go if the doors are open," because they were not. He did not say, "Go if you have an invitation or are welcomed." He said, "Go," because people need His Word. (Piper 1986:237)

Those behind veils are waiting for a friend. Will you go?

9

No Greater Love: 21st Century Martyrs
David McDonnall (1975-2004)
Larry Elliot (1943-2004)
Jean Elliot (1945-2004)
Karen Watson (1965-2004)

On March 15, 2004, as their truck bounced along the dusty road, David, Carrie, Larry, Jean, and Karen talked about their day. As relief workers in Iraq, they were tired, but excited after a day of surveying possible areas for water purification projects. Iraqis around the city of Mosul in northern Iraq had welcomed them warmly and had invited them to return soon. But as they approached the ancient ruins of Nineveh, a truck pulled alongside them and opened fire with machine guns. Four of the five were killed! David, Larry, Jean, and Karen paid the ultimate price. They laid down their lives for their friends:

the Iraqi people. Unlike the prophet Jonah who ran away when God called, these five volunteered for this dangerous assignment. What was it that brought this relief team together? Who were these 21st century martyrs?

He went places where no outsider had dared go before to share the gospel. He walked through minefields and worked in the midst of civil wars to find lost villages. He got arrested in three countries for telling people about Jesus. He became friends with Bedouins (Arab tribesmen from ancient times). He traveled across the desert of North Africa. He enjoyed life! To David McDonnall, life was an adventure, but it was an adventure with a purpose! David's purpose was to bring unreached nations into a relationship with the living God. For this adventure, David risked his life many times, and finally, gave up his life on a dusty road in northern Iraq.

David was born February 24, 1975, in Colorado Springs, Colorado. He accepted Jesus as his Lord and Savior when he was seven years old. "His relationship with Christ from the earliest days was always the number one thing in his life," says his mother. While in high school, he was shy and spent much time by himself. He enjoyed hiking in the mountains, photography, fishing, and hunting. David was a very good student. He received an academic scholarship for college and majored in photography and journalism.

At college, he became known as "Dangerous Dave." He knew how to have fun, but not get involved in immoral or bad things. According to his friends, Dave did not seem to need much sleep. He would stay up all night, knock on dorm room doors, and ask his friends to go rappelling or hiking at three in the morning. David's energy, enthusiasm, and leadership abilities combined to make him a natural leader for student mission trips and witnessing teams. His friend Shawn says, "He was a servant. People were always calling him. It didn't matter if he was busy or not. If somebody needed something, he was there to help." (Bridges 2005:137)

After college graduation he worked at a newspaper and was soon promoted to news editor. But David was restless. He wanted more from life. A two-week mission trip to the country of Tanzania changed his life. David returned from this trip with a deepened commitment to follow Christ wherever He led and with an urgency to take the gospel to the unreached.

About that time, a worker among Muslims was looking for a few adventurous young people to go to North Africa and the Middle East. The plan was daring! The teams would wander through some of the most difficult, dangerous parts of the region and find openings for the gospel. "These guys were going to go where nobody had ever gone," the missionary stated. David was the first to sign up!

Sent out in 1998, Dave moved to the North Africa/ Middle East region. He learned the language quickly and made many friends. Arabs and other North Africans loved this friendly, talkative, funny guy from America. Wherever he went, people remembered him. During the next two years, Dave and his partner Chad had many adventures, crossing deserts, surviving sand storms, and sharing the gospel with many who had never heard. They did not see any converts, but their work made it possible for others to follow. Dave and Chad were directly involved in the beginning of a church-planting effort that produced more than 150 churches by 2004.

Dave was arrested and questioned in one country while surveying. He was detained by secret police in another country while distributing the *Jesus* film. Once, men waving AK-47s held him and Chad for hours. This "danger" was worth it to Dave. He loved Arabs. He wanted to tell them about the God who had given him that love. A friend remembers, "We would always talk about if we did not share God's love with Muslims, then who would?" (Bridges 2005:144) Dave just couldn't understand how people could stay in America while there was such a need in other countries.

A year into his assignment, Dave and another team member went to Bethlehem on December 31, 1999, to celebrate the turn of the millennium. That night, he met another worker among Muslims named Carrie Taylor. They were amazed at the things they shared in common, particularly their burden and love for the Arab world.

After the completion of their two-year terms in 2001, they enrolled in seminary, and were married the next year. They were involved in a local church and remained passionate about reaching the nations with the gospel.

In the spring of 2003, American, British, and coalition forces overthrew Saddam Hussein's long-ruling dictatorship in Iraq. The initial part of the war ended in a few months, as Iraqi forces collapsed. But the Iraqi people needed help to recover. Hunger, poverty, and lack of clean water were just some of the problems.

Despite the dangers, secular and religious groups began to respond. Southern Baptist churches packed and sent thousands of boxes of food to be given around the country. Relief workers and volunteers delivered the food to needy families and made friends. In June of that year, Dave and Carrie led an 18-member team of volunteers to Iraq.

After their return from the volunteer trip, Carrie said, "We both wanted to be overseas serving as missionaries more than anything, because that is where our heart was." (Bridges 2005:148) However, they did not have immediate plans to return. But in the early fall, an unexpected and urgent call came from a mission organization: *Would they consider returning as soon as possible, to help coordinate relief projects in northern Iraq for a year?* After praying and fasting, they both were challenged from God's Word to "give everything and go." They returned eager to help Iraqis rebuild their lives.

Larry Elliot was a big man with a big laugh. Jean, his wife, was known for giving many hugs. "Whatever it takes" was how Larry lived his life. Jean's main thing was building relationships. Larry could make things happen. He could come up with a solution. Jean (and Larry) loved children, and helped hundreds of them in various ways. They had always worked together with total commitment to each other and to the Lord. They would die, as they had lived.

Larry was born during World War II on a tobacco farm in North Carolina. He grew up knowing how to plow and plant.

He received the Lord at the age of nine, was involved in church, and as a youth, occasionally preached. Larry served in the United States Army in Germany and in Vietnam. After returning home from Vietnam, he became a manager of a factory and served the Lord through his local church.

Jean was born in 1945, the seventh of eight children of Robert and Irene Dover. Both of Jean's parents worked in a factory. They did not have much money, but Mrs. Dover took time to teach her children about the Lord. "Second Baptist Church was a vital part of my life," Jean wrote of her early years. "I have always attended church since my infancy. My mother would talk with our family about the Bible. She not only talked about the Bible, she obeyed the Bible. I am grateful to God for being blessed with a Christian mother." (Bridges 2005:163) Jean, like Larry, accepted the Lord when she was nine years old. Friends and family remember that Jean was a special child. She always wanted to be a missionary, even when she was a little girl.

Larry and Jean met in college and married. It was while Larry was in Vietnam that God reminded Jean of her calling to be a missionary. Larry surrendered to missions several years later. He said that after he committed his life completely to the Lord, "I knew I had to resign my job that day and enter seminary." (Bridges 2005:167) That is what he did! Larry earned a degree from the seminary and Jean completed the requirements for appointment as missionaries.

In 1978, Larry and Jean became Southern Baptist missionaries and served in Honduras for 25 years. Larry was a very practical person with a deep love for people. The physical needs of Honduras were so overwhelming that Larry began to see many ways to show God's love to Hondurans. Their first major community development project focused on a community of 200 homes. There was not one usable latrine in the whole village! Larry and Jean mobilized people and resources, held medical and dental clinics, treated hundreds of patients, helped build latrines, taught basic hygiene, and held evangelistic services at night. This project also helped in providing clean water for all the community's 1,500 people. The project was such a success that Larry's direction for life was set. He began to reach out to many isolated, hungry, and disaster-prone areas of Honduras through relief and development ministries.

Larry studied geology, agriculture, parasitology; anything it took to help the people in their suffering and poverty. However, as time went on, Larry realized one thing was needed in most places: clean water. Beginning with a little knowledge and using a small, donated well-drilling rig, he became an expert on the subject.

Jean often went with Larry on his trips into the country. However, she developed her own varied ministries of love. She cared about people. She built relationships. Jean taught English. She discipled Honduran women. She opened her home. She prayed and prayed! Jean would go into the slums and teach people how to read and cook. She provided reading glasses for hundreds of people. Both Larry and Jean provided many scholarships to enable Honduran children to attend school, buy textbooks, and buy school uniforms.

In their 26 years of ministry in Honduras, they left behind 80 water wells, 12 Baptist churches, and 92 mission points (Bible studies that are developing into churches). Some thought it was foolish to consider leaving a successful ministry. With just a few years left until retirement, "Why did they have to go and put themselves in the middle of a shooting war?" However, when the Elliots watched the news and saw the people struggling to survive in Iraq, God began to speak to them. One day, Larry saw a TV report showing old Iraqi men dipping buckets in dirty water for something to drink. "I could help them," he told himself.

Soon after, Larry was asked to go to southern Iraq. It was so dangerous; they wore helmets and bulletproof jackets! But Larry gladly went. He had not been there long when he knew "God had laid that country on his heart." After much prayer, Larry and Jean were convinced they needed to go to Iraq. While they planned for their move, friends and family urged them to go someplace, any place but Iraq. Larry's response was honest. "Yes, we could get killed." Jean told her daughter, with tears rolling down her cheeks, "We are going to a dark place and we are taking the light of Jesus." In spite of the danger, they were excited to put their long experience to full use for needy Iraqis.

The letter, written over a year before Karen Watson died, said it all. Like a soldier, she had signed her name, not knowing the future. She had sealed the letter, and written these words on the outside: "Open in case of death." Karen sold or gave away everything that would not fit in a duffel bag. Now she was ready to go. As her plane left America to go to the Middle East, she wrote in her journal: "For the sake of the call. Reckless abandon. Abandon it all. No other reason at all." Karen had not always loved the Lord or lived her life so passionately.

Karen Denise Watson was born June 18, 1965. Her parents divorced when she was a child. Her father was not there for her. She had a lot of hurt and loneliness during her childhood. Karen's sister took care of her because their mother was busy working.

As Karen grew into adulthood, tragedy struck three times. First, in 1985, a drunk driver killed her grandmother whom she loved very much. Later, Karen re-established contact with her father and their relationship was reconciled. But he, too, was killed in 1987. At this time, Karen met a man and they fell in love. He treated her like a queen. He was romantic, sending her flowers and gifts. She had never had this kind of affection before. He made her feel secure. They were engaged and excited about the future. Karen also grew very close to his parents. Her dream of a happy family was about to come true. Then, in a horrible attack, a crazy member of her fiance's family murdered him and his parents. It was too much to bear. Karen could take no more heartbreak.

A Christian friend reached out to Karen. She took care of her during her darkest days. It was during this time that Karen wrote, "I opened my heart (to a believer) about wanting to know Jesus and how scared I was. We talked on the phone for two and a half hours. I asked God to be my Savior and come into my life. The next morning my very first thought was of the Lord! I was so happy." Karen's hurts would take many years to heal, but after accepting Jesus, she was a new person. She wrote later, "How wonderful it was for me to find the love of Jesus envelop me when I thought there was no hope left. I remember feeling like the weight of the world was lifted off of my shoulders. He gave me a new heart that grew a love it had never known possible. I was hungry for God's word and for fellowship with His people." (Bridges 2005:200)

Karen got involved in church, began to witness, and led many people to the Lord. She loved kids and taught Vacation Bible School. She became very active in missions education in her church and helped raise money for missionaries. She also took time off from work to visit the Holy Land and go on mission trips to Mexico, El Salvador, Kosovo, Macedonia, and Greece. After her second trip to El Salvador, she penned these words: "What will I do with the rest of my life? Serve the world? Or serve God? Go into ministry? Go to the mission field?" (Bridges 2005:205) As the months passed and her burden grew, she realized more clearly that God was calling her to go to the lost and hurting.

The war in Iraq looked certain and Christian workers were already anticipating that, when the war was over, the Iraqi people would need much help to recover. A team leader from the region wrote a job description for an aid-relief coordinator to be based in the area. When the team leader outlined the job for Karen, which included working under pressure, developing contacts and effective relationships with Iraqi officials, coordinating food aid and relief supply shipments, starting building projects and assist in placement of other workers and volunteers, she responded without delay: "Let's do it!" Karen set up an office in Kuwait and waited until they could go into Iraq. She worked long, long hours attending meetings with government and United Nations officials, etc.

Within weeks after the fall of Saddam Hussein's regime, Karen was in Baghdad with the first wave of relief workers. She coordinated all workers coming in, obtaining lodging and workspace, hiring drivers and guards, and monitoring security. Karen worked with others to help distribute thousands of food boxes sent by Southern Baptist churches and to help rebuild damaged schools. She ministered to widows, met with educated women, and reached out to the women in her neighborhood. She wrote, "I have met some special ladies in my neighborhood who just want someone to talk to and have tea with. They want to tell their story of pain. They just feel so free. I want for them the real freedom of our Lord." (Bridges 2005:211)

As time passed, the spiritual battle became more and more real for Karen and her co-workers. The terrorist network was becoming more organized, and threats against foreigners were increasing. Karen was almost killed several times in Baghdad. After the U.N. headquarters was bombed in Baghdad, she wrote, "The horror of it all. How many will die?

I think of their eternity. We all know people there (who died in the bombing) we just keep going." (Bridges 2005:212) Karen kept going, but she was burning out. The pressure was too great. In September 2003, Karen asked permission to leave.

While away, she rested, prayed, and studied key passages from the Bible. She confronted her fears with these truths: "Rejoice to the extent that you partake of Christ's sufferings, that when His glory is revealed, you may also be glad with exceeding joy" (1 Pet. 4:13 NKJV). "Our light affliction, which is but for a moment, is working for us a far more exceeding and eternal weight of glory" (2 Cor. 4:17 NKJV). We are created to be in the likeness of His Son Jesus. The normal Christian life, according to the apostle Paul, was one of suffering. She was ready to go back.

Dave and Carrie gave everything and went. Larry and Jean knew it was dangerous and dark. Karen had written her own epitaph. Five lives had been brought together for one purpose: being a friend and showing love to the sons of Ishmael in the land of Nineveh.

Larry, Jean, and Karen died instantly. David spent his last few minutes helping his critically injured wife. Carrie survived, but it would be months before she could walk again. At the 2004 Southern Baptist Convention, before thousands of people, she challenged the listeners, "We have to keep going to the hard places. We have to keep going to the violent places."

Karen Watson's Letter

Dear Pastor Phil and Pastor Roger,
You should only be reading this in the event of death.
When God calls there are no regrets. I tried to share my heart
with you as much as possible, my heart for the nations. I was
not called to a place; I was called to Him. To obey was my
objective, to suffer was expected, His glory, my reward, His
glory, my reward…

The missionary heart:
Cares more than some think is wise
Risks more than some think is safe
Dreams more than some think is practical
Expects more than some think is possible
I was called not to comfort or to success but to obedience..
There is no joy outside of knowing Jesus and serving Him.

David McDonnall, Larry Elliot,
Jean Elliot, Karen Watson

10

The New ISLAM– "I Sincerely Love All Muslims" The Story of Rev. Florentino de Jesus (1910-1998)
by Josil C. Gonzales

It was September 1998. The whole country was caught up in the frenzy of the 100th year anniversary celebration of the Philippine Independence. It was a time for remembering heroes. I was attending a meeting in Davao City in preparation for a big conference for Mission to Muslim (M2M) workers. It was there that we received the sad news that "Rev. Florentino de Jesus has just died." "Tatay de Jesus" or the "Grand Old Man" as he was fondly called, had been a pioneer among M2M workers. He was the patriarch of the CAMACOP (Christian and Missionary Alliance Churches of the Philippines). He was 88. There was a moment of silence. Then an American missionary warmly commented, "Now we have a genuine Filipino hero we can all be proud of."

Rev. de Jesus' life and accomplishments continue to inspire men and women working among Muslims. He is warmly regarded as a life model to a new generation of Filipino M2M workers. In a recent meeting among M2M leaders, the misunderstanding and tension between workers based in Manila and those in Mindanao was being discussed. One leader sighed and said, "If only Rev. de Jesus were here with us..." Another quickly added, "And that is almost like having the Holy Spirit on our side." We all nodded and smiled in agreement.

De Jesus was born on October 16, 1910 to a Christian family in Davao City. His father, Antonio Sr., was the first Protestant pastor of the Congregational church in the city. He was also a former officer of the Spanish army. One incident changed the life of their growing family. A drunken man assaulted De Jesus' sisters at home and his father, Antonio Sr., had no choice but to shoot the assailant. The drunken man fell dead to the floor. For that, Antonio Sr. was sent to the San Ramon Penal Colony in Zamboanga City.

However, because of his good behavior, Antonio Sr. was appointed as the trustee of the prison. The whole family joined him there. They were now all together again. But their bliss was short-lived. De Jesus' mother died while giving birth to another son, Antonio Jr.

Her death marked the start of a wild life for Florentino and his other brother, Jose. The two brothers skipped their classes and got involved in much mischief. Concerned about his misbehaving sons, Antonio Sr. thought that whipping them was the solution. However, the more he whipped them, the more the boys became bitter. They ran away from home so many times they became known as "The Runaway Boys."

The year 1926 was a turning point in the life of 16-year-old Florentino. He attended an evangelistic meeting conducted by Rev. JD Williams, a Christian and Missionary Alliance (C&MA) missionary. Years later, Florentino would say, "I do not remember...the passage of Scripture used to point me to Christ the Savior. One thing, though, I vividly recall is that from that day in 1926, my life took a new direction, a new meaning. The old was passing away! Love for God, my loved ones and my friends began to possess my heart."

In 1927, while finishing his intermediate studies, Florentino was stricken with tuberculosis. He was given only three months to live. He managed to survive after three months but he was still sick. "Would you like to try Jesus, the Great Physician, for divine healing?" a missionary asked him. He said yes. The missionary, together with another missionary, laid their hands on him and prayed for healing in the name of Jesus Christ. Nothing happened at first. But in desperation, Florentino promised, "Lord, if You will be pleased to spare my life, I'll serve You as long as I live." God answered his prayer by healing him.

When the Ebenezer Bible Institute was established in 1928 in Zamboanga City, Florentino enrolled as a freshman in the four-year course of Theology. In his sophomore year, the school deployed students to various places to minister. Florentino could never forget what the school principal said, "We are going to enter Sulu and reach the Muslims for the Lord."

"Lord, send us anywhere but Sulu!" was the fervent prayer of most students at Ebenezer, including Florentino.

After his graduation in 1931, he married his childhood sweetheart, Maria Pada, on July 1 of that same year. They were sent to Siasi for their first church assignment. Thus began their exciting 60-year adventure of ministering to Muslims. Through the years, the couple and their four children were preserved and protected from dangers and difficult circumstances. The following stories are just a few of such instances.

When the Japanese forces occupied Jolo in December 1942, Florentino and his family, along with other families and friends, were living on Siasi. They had to flee to Sisangat island. Eventually, all the missionaries left the island except for Florentino and his family. God, through Psalm 37, had told them to stay. They settled in a floating village of about 2,000 stilt houses and remained God's soldiers on this lonely outpost.

Like the apostle Paul, the de Jesus family faced danger many times. Fleeing persecution, they transferred from one house to another. One time, some American pilots were shot down by the Japanese and were rescued by Sama fishermen. In spite of the danger to his life, Florentino led in planning for the pilots' escape. A native sailboat was commandeered for their use, a meager meal also prepared for them and a special prayer offered for their safety. "Forming themselves into a circle and with hands clasped to each other, the entire de Jesus family sang for them the hymns 'God will take care of you' and 'God be with you till we meet again.'" As the sailboat slowly moved away from the de Jesus home, bound for Australia, the pilots all stood, took off their hats and bowed their heads.

The days went by and the family was forced to ration their food and water. Their diet consisted of dried fish, peanuts and cassava. They were totally dependent on rain for their drinking water. Books sent to de Jesus by a former missionary before the war broke out were heaven sent. *By My Spirit, The Life of George Müller* and *Streams in the Desert* became a real help to Florentino in the bitter days of the Occupation. Compared to Müller, he considered himself a "kindergarten student" in the school of prayer and faith. But somehow he was encouraged to hold on to God even when contacts with the outside world were completely cut off. Müller's life was a challenge to him particularly when the cassava and fresh water supply for the family was touching bottom. Hearing God. Perseverance in the midst of difficulties and persecution. Childlike trust. God's faithfulness. Love for Muslims. The war years had taught him much about himself and about God. Florentino had gone through the fire and had come out stronger. He realized that these trials served to purify him for a greater task.

His impressive ministry, dedication and longevity to the work among the Muslims resulted in his partnership with Open Doors from 1973 to 1976. Florentino was asked to develop a pioneering program to reach out to the Muslims in the south and those studying in Manila. In December 1978, the first Love Your Neighbor conference was held in Zamboanga City. The mere fact that the meeting took place was amazing because it was not yet popular at that time to speak of a ministry among Muslims.

The success of this endeavor prompted Open Doors to encourage him to form his own mission group entirely committed to making Christ known among the Muslims in the Philippines. In May 1979, the Love Your Neighbor Inc. or LYN (formerly called Operation Love Muslims) was established in Zamboanga City. After three years, LYN launched out on its own.

Rev. de Jesus was also responsible for bringing the M2M work to the popular consciousness of the Filipino Evangelical Church. He persevered in the work when others had given up. It was his constant and consistent appeals for more workers that attracted more people to come and work in the various parts of Southern Philippines.

In 1989 at the Lausanne Parallel Congress, he gave a challenge where more than a hundred participants responded. Many of them are now key players in the outreach to Muslims here in the Philippines and across Asia. Some have become the leaders of major mission organizations, churches, and foundations, which now champion the cause of M2M work.

No one can measure the result of that one meeting. Literally hundreds and thousands of believers have become friends of Ishmael, as the ripple effect continues. Cross-cultural workers continue to be sent out. Thousands, if not hundreds of thousands, of Muslims have been blessed because of Rev. Florentino de Jesus and the 1989 Lausanne Parallel Congress.

In 1994, after hearing Rev. de Jesus' appeal for more workers, one pastor left his church to minister among the sons of Ishmael. His personal goal that first year was to win one Muslim to the Lord and to disciple him. At the end of the year, he reported that he was not able to meet this simple goal. For several years he sought to accomplish the same goal but still witnessed no response. It took five years before his work was blessed with its first Muslim background believer (MBB).

Many times work among Muslims is difficult. The response is either slow or none at all. God is calling out a generation who will take up their cross and follow Christ to the hard places. It will not be easy! God's call is for people to minister as goers for life, to live among a people, and learn their language and culture. The task cannot be finished on a one-month short-term trip! God desires a deep commitment to His Great Commission and the Greatest Commandment. This commitment means giving up our resources in order that the sons of Ishmael might come to Christ. One missionary reported that after seven years of work in a city in Southern Philippines and two other areas in the region among three large mission agencies with six missionary couples, only two Filipino Muslims became believers.

Although I had known Rev. de Jesus since the late '70s, I had never had the privilege of working with him until October 1996. He had just returned from a four-year sojourn in Canada. He was 86 years old. Even though his body showed signs of weakness, his passion and zeal for Muslims was undiminished and unwavering. His eyesight may have dimmed, but his vision remained clear and steadfast. Rev. de Jesus began what he called his "R and R mission–revival among Christians and reconciliation with the Muslims." He just kept going and going and going.

During an interview with Rev. de Jesus last May 1997, he gave credit to Open Doors for being fundamental in the establishment and continuance of LYN's ministry to this day. "Without Open Doors, LYN would not be in existence today," he acknowledged. In a letter dated February 10, 1997, he wrote, "Thank you for Open Doors' contribution (towards our projects). Only eternity will reveal the impact that Open Doors has made in the spread of the gospel to Muslims worldwide."

I was privileged to give a eulogy at Rev. de Jesus' funeral service at the Ebenezer Community Alliance Church in Zamboanga City on September 25, 1998. Among other things, I said, "When I came in yesterday afternoon to pay respects to the remains of Tatay, the de Jesus clan was practicing on stage their special number to be rendered today. I hesitated to enter the chapel, because I might be intruding into something private. But when they told me to come up front, through their smiles and beckoning hands, I came. I stood in front of Tatay's coffin. As I was staring at his unmoving face, the de Jesus family members began to sing. I couldn't help but look at their faces one by one. And I told myself, 'Tatay can now rest in peace because 18 of his heirs are here to continue the work.'" These were my closing remarks: "Let me just say that I would not say goodbye to Tatay. As a noted writer, C.S. Lewis has pointed out, 'Christians don't say goodbye, they just say, 'See you later.'"

Yes, we now have a genuine Filipino hero of the faith. In our present time when contemporary heroes are hard to come by, when our political leaders cease to be persons of virtue and integrity, it is refreshing to know that we have Tatay de Jesus whom we can all emulate and follow. His life inspires us, and pushes us to give our very best in whatever circumstances we may find ourselves. Rev. de Jesus remained faithful and fruitful for over 60 years to his Master and to his motto, "The New ISLAM" (I Sincerely Love All Muslims).

Yes, thank you, Tatay, for being a friend to the sons of Ishmael. And see you later!

Section 4

11

Beliefs and Practices of Islam

As I write this chapter, I am sitting in a hotel room in a city with many Muslims. I am attending a youth mission congress, in which the emphasis is to reach out to the unreached people groups, including Muslims. As I have walked to the meetings or ridden on public transportation, I have met these friendly people on the road and have sat next to them. This close contact has not been as scary as I thought it would be. I want to say so much to them, but I do not know where or how to start. Becoming a friend to Ishmael is new for me, as I know it is for many of you.

Up to this point in the book, I have given you a little history and a lot of inspiration. Hopefully, as you have read about these past and present heroes of the faith, something down deep in your heart has cried out, "Yes, I want to do more. I want to become a friend to Muslims." In order to become a true friend to Muslims, you must take time to really know who they are and what they believe. In this section of the book, I will give you some practical information that will help you get started.

The Pillars of Islam

The first and last words whispered in a Muslim's ear are "There is no god but God (Allah), and Muhammad is his messenger." This confession, or *Shahada*, is the foundation of their faith. It is the entry point into the life of Islam. It is the first of the five pillars of Islam. This belief in one God is called *Tawhid*. To the Muslim, God is the all-powerful creator, the sovereign ruler, and the sustainer of the universe. There is none like him. Many Muslims believe that Allah does not have personal fellowship with man. He is absolutely one and without equal. The interpretation of the absolute oneness of God rules out any possibility for the Trinity. However, it must be noted that many Muslims believe that the Christian doctrine of the Trinity is God, Mary, and Jesus as found in Al Qur'an 5:116. A Muslim is one who "submits all of his or her life to the commands of the one and only God." God's laws, as recorded in the Qur'an, rule every aspect of a Muslim's life.

The second pillar of Islam is the ritual prayer, or *Salat*. Before the sun rises, "Allahu Akbar... Allahu Akbar" can be heard blaring from loudspeakers of the local mosques. Five times a day Muslims are called to prayer: dawn, midmorning, noon, afternoon, and finally in the evening. This call, translated from Arabic, says something like this:

> God is most great. God is most great.
> God is most great. God is most great.

I testify that there is no god except God.

I testify that there is no god except God.

I testify that Muhammad is the messenger of God.

I testify that Muhammad is the messenger of God.

Come to Prayer! Come to Prayer!

Come to success! (in this life and the hereafter)

Come to success!

God is the most great. God is the most great.

There is no god except God. (Marshall 2002:19-20)

Every time this call is heard, Muslims (mainly men, because women are not required to attend the time of prayer) are expected to stop whatever they are doing and go immediately to the mosque. If they are not near a mosque, Muslims unroll a prayer rug and pray wherever they are. These prayers are always directed toward the Ka'aba in Mecca. The prayer time is a ritual of standing, kneeling, and bowing. The Muslim is required to be solemn. They are also not allowed to talk to each other. Each prayer consists of reciting the first Sura (chapter) of the Qur'an, followed by other chosen verses and praises to God.

Mandatory giving or *Zakat* is the third pillar of Islam. Simply put, *Zakat* is a 2.5 percent tax on everything owned, not just income, given to the mosque at the end of the year. The money is then given to those who need it, as dictated by the Qur'an. Since there is no separation of church and state in Muslim-dominated governments, this money also provides for the state and the community.

The fourth pillar of Islam is the observance of Ramadan or *Sawm*. Ramadan is both a fast and a feast. It takes place during the ninth month of the Islamic calendar, remembering and celebrating the giving of the Qur'an to the prophet Muhammad. During this month, Muslims fast from before dawn to dusk. They are required to abstain from all food and drink, sexual intercourse, and other actions considered inappropriate.

The Pilgrimage or *hajj* to Mecca is the fifth pillar of Islam. A Muslim, who is physically and financially able, is required to take this pilgrimage to the holy places in and around Mecca. The Ka'aba is the most important site. The Ka'aba is an ancient cube-shaped building where the black stone, which Muhammad left after destroying all of the idols in Mecca in AD 632, is kept. Islam teaches that Abraham and Hagar visited Mecca. Muslims also believe that the Ka'aba was originally founded by Adam and his son Seth, and later rebuilt by Abraham and Ishmael.

Many would include *Jihad*, or Holy War as a sixth pillar of Islam. It literally means, "Struggle on behalf of God." Muslim extremists interpret *Jihad* as God's command to kill or conquer all Zionists (Jews) and infidels (United States, Great Britain, and the West). Moderate and secular Muslims interpret *Jihad* as the struggle to be better and do better according to the will of God. Muslims who die as martyrs while involved in *Jihad* are guaranteed eternal life.

Basic Beliefs of Islam and Christianity Compared

(See chart in Appendix)

Different "Denominations" or Sects of Islam

Muslims, at times, will ask why there are so many different groups of Christians. Rightly so, the division and lack of love shown at times among Christians have confused Muslims and kept them from knowing the true gospel of Jesus Christ. However, neither can Muslims claim that Islam is unified. Khalid Duran, in his book, *Children of Abraham,* claims that Islam has 73 different sects. (Marshall 2002:26-27) In this book, I will only deal with five of these groups within Islam.

The Sunni are the largest Muslim group. They make up 85% of all Muslims. They are dedicated to the authority of the Islamic written material. They follow the Qur'an, the *Sunna* (the behavior and practice of Muhammad in Medina), and the *Hadith* (Muhammad's spoken decisions and judgments). An Orthodox Sunni would want to live under *Shariah* Law. This type of Muslim could probably be compared to the Orthodox Jew in Jesus' day, seeking to please God by living strictly by the law.

The Shi'a live mainly in Iran and Iraq. They comprise about 15% of the Muslim population. They believe that the leader of the worldwide community of Islam should come from the family of the Prophet, thus having "prophetic authority." Because of this direct connection to Muhammad, Shiites believe that their leader, or Imam, has the authority to interpret the Qur'an and lead the Muslim community perfectly. They have been known throughout Islam's history as protestors.

A third main group in Islam is known as the Sufis. These Muslims are seeking a deeper, more mystical, religious experience or a personal relationship with Allah. They often minimize the formalism and the legalistic aspects of Islam. They believe they can receive revelations from God. They can belong to either the Sunni or Shiite sects, and are often persecuted within Islam.

Folk Islam, like folk Christianity and folk Buddhism, is a mixture of high religion and low religion. High religion in Islam is the five pillars practiced by all faithful Muslims. These five pillars are easily learned and recognized. Major Islamic beliefs such as the absolute oneness of God, the authority of the Qur'an, belief in angels or *Jiin* would also be considered high religion. Low religion is characterized by pagan beliefs and magical practices. This mixing of high religion and low religion is called syncretism.

According to Phil Parshall, 70% of all Islamic people are folk Muslims. (Van Rheenen 1991:27) That is, they are Muslim by name and culture, follow the requirements of Islam outwardly, but their core belief system is still pagan. For example, many Muslims use the confession of faith to counter the forces of the *evil eye* and to drive away evil spirits; the words become power instead of a confession of faith. Folk Muslims say prayers, give alms, fast during Ramadan, and go on the pilgrimage in order to gain *Baraka*. *Baraka* is an impersonal spiritual power defined as blessing, grace, and mercy. *Baraka* protects from danger and gives charisma or power to leaders. Folk Muslims view *Baraka* as a magical force, which can be obtained through ritual and manipulation. Other folk Islamic practices are the worship of *Pirs* (mystical religious guides who serve as mediators between god and man) and Zar ceremonies, in which spirits are called into practitioners for the purpose of divination. The Bible refers to these practitioners as *spiritist* or *mediums*. God's Word says, "Let no one be found among you who…practices sorcery, interprets omens, engages in witchcraft, or casts spells, or who is a medium or a spiritist or who consults the dead" (Deut. 18:10, 11).

Therefore, to effectively bring God's blessing of salvation to Muslims, there must be a *truth encounter*. We must present the gospel to Muslims in a culturally sensitive way so they are really confronted with the truth. This *truth encounter* is an attack on the errors of Islamic beliefs. However, there must also be a *power encounter*. The gospel must touch Muslims at the core of their lives. We must answer the questions that Muslims are asking about life, sickness, fear, evil spirits, crops, etc. A *power encounter* is a visible demonstration of the power of God, which proves the gospel message we are preaching. As Paul and Barnabas went into Gentile areas, the Lord "confirmed the message of grace by enabling them to do miraculous signs and wonders" (Acts 14:3). Because of this, many believed. May we go out ready to preach the truth, but may we also go out ready to establish the kingdom of God in the fullness of the Holy Spirit.

Islamic Radicals

Since the attack on the World Trade Center on September 11, 2001, Osama bin Laden has been the one most connected with radical Islam. Al Qaeda has become a common household word. However, there is little understanding of this extreme movement. Al Qaeda's official name is the *World Islamic Front for Holy War against Jews and Crusaders*. Al Qaeda was officially organized in 1998 to form a network of worldwide terrorist organizations. At one time, it had cells in over 60 countries and has been involved in violence in over a dozen countries.

There are many factors in the rise of radical Islam. Rick Love, in an article entitled *Faces of Islam: A Christian Perspective* lists that:

1. Muslims, like Christians, reject materialism, pornography and high divorce rate. Some Muslim leaders call America the "Great Satan," because of its influence in spreading these negative values.

2. Radical Islamic movements perceive the United States and the West as being responsible for the deaths of many Muslims. They cite the United States' support of Israel, while ignoring the plight of the Palestinians and Lebanese. The Serbian/Bosnian war is another case in point where nominal Christians slaughtered thousands of Muslims. The West did not intervene. Many Muslims now criticize the invasion and occupation of Iraq.

3. Radical Islam has grown because of controlled and biased media in many Muslim countries.

4. Muslims believe they should be the dominant force in the world. But the reality is that 80 % of the world's poorest people are Muslims. Two-thirds of all refugees in the world are Muslims. The radical Muslim does not like it that the West still has political, economic, technological, media and moral power.

5. Many Muslims are outraged because of the presence of U.S. troops in Saudi Arabia, the heart of Islam.

Much of the radical ideology being taught among the fundamentalists comes from three movements within Islam. One of these movements is called *Wahhabism*, following the teaching of Muhammad ibn Abd al-Wahhab. He lived in Central Arabia from about 1703 until 1792. He strictly followed the Qur'an, persecuting and fighting other Muslims to force them to submit to his version of Islam. For al-Wahhab, it was a religious duty to put to death anyone who strayed from his version of Islam. The Saud tribe adopted his views and eventually came to power in Arabia, establishing the kingdom of Saudi Arabia. Wahhabism now has been spread all over the world through the establishment of thousands of schools *(madrassas)*.

The Muslim Brotherhood is another radical movement in Islam, which was started in Egypt by Hassan al-Banna (1906-1949). He opposed the Egyptian government, saying they had compromised and were following the West. Their next leader, Sayyid Outb (1906-1966) also attacked Christianity, Jews, capitalism, materialism, and the role of women. Through his writings, Outb became one of the most influential Muslim writers of the 20th century. He urged Muslims to fight against the West and against their own corrupt Muslim leaders. The Brotherhood continues today and has developed into many different movements.

Radical Shiites

The name most associated with this movement is the Ayatollah Khomeini (1902-1989). In the 1970s, he called for a *Jihad* against the ruler of Iran and, in 1979, successfully overthrew the government. He created a regime where the Muslim religious leaders controlled everything. Since then, they have openly called on Muslims throughout the world to turn their mosques into military bases in order to conduct *Jihad* against the crusaders and Jews. They have founded terrorism groups such as Hezbollah and even recently, their new leader called for the destruction of Israel.

Radical Islam's goal is to spread their version of Islam to the whole world. If you are still in doubt concerning their version of Islam, read again about Afghanistan under the Taliban. Do some research about the country of Sudan since radical Islamists took power in a 1985 coup. Take a look at Iran's government since the Islamic revolution in 1979.

In defense of the majority of Muslims who are peace-loving, it must be made clear that radical Islam's acts of terror not only target Christians and Jews, but also Muslim nations "who have compromised with the West or with the radical's interpretation and application of Islamic law." In other words, anyone who does not agree with the radical's interpretation of

Islam must be conquered or eliminated.

Therefore, as one writer states, "Islam itself is at a crossroad." (Marshall 2002:109) Moderate Muslims must speak up now or risk being silenced later by the militant Muslims. The world is also at a crossroad. World governments who believe in peace and freedom must use force to stop terrorism, whether it is terrorism done by Hindus, Buddhists, Christians, or Muslims. Terrorism is terrorism.

I also believe that the followers of Jesus Christ stand at a crossroad. The prophet Jeremiah said, "Stand at the crossroad and look." Look! Through Saudi oil money, Islam is actively starting relief organizations, hospitals, publishing material, starting schools, universities, funding teachers, building mosques, and sending missionaries to other countries. "Stand at the crossroad and look." Where are the followers of Jesus spending their money? American Christians last year spent more money on dog food than on missions. Filipino Christians spent more money on phone cards than on missions. "Stand at the crossroad and look." Islam is spreading rapidly among the tribal people of Africa. Where are the Christians who are willing to go where the road is hard or where there is no road at all? "Stand at the crossroad and look." Radical Muslims are willing to die for what they believe! Where are the followers of Jesus who are willing to lay down their lives for the sake of the gospel?

Crossroads always require a decision. Are you ready to be a friend to Ishmael?

12

Sharing the Gospel with the Sons of Ishmael

Dar al-Islam or the "House of Islam" is divided into 49 countries, representing 77% of all Muslims. The other 23% live as minorities in other lands. Furthermore, Muslims are divided into 408 different major ethnic groups. As we have seen in Chapter 11, Muslims are also very different in their understanding and applying the teachings of the Qur'an. Therefore, it is impossible to find the "one correct way" to share the gospel with a Muslim. In a short book like this, it is also impossible to present, in detail, every good method being used today to bring God's blessing to Muslims. In this chapter, I will present some basic principles in sharing the gospel, the cost in following Christ for Muslims, the need for contextualization, and a summary of specific approaches.

The Greatest of These is Love

Love is the greatest strategy a believer has for sharing the gospel with a Muslim. More are won by love than by debate. Divine love is missing from Islam, therefore they need to know and see that God is love. God *so loved* the world that *He gave* His only Son to die. We are told from the Scriptures that we did not seek God first, but because of His love, He looked for us. As we come into a relationship with God, through Jesus Christ, His love is poured out into our hearts. We are commanded to "live a life of love" (Eph. 5:2), "put on love" (Col. 3:14), and that the "only thing that counts is faith expressing itself in love" (Gal. 5:6).

Easier said than done! Love when you are hated? Love when no one listens? Love when there are no results? Love Muslims when they have been your enemy for years? Yes. Love. If you are having trouble with this command to love, then stop and meditate on these ten reasons we should love Muslims.

1. *God loves Muslims!* Muslims are loved by God in the same way that He loves all people. Like all humans, Muslims are created in the image of God (Gen. 1:26-27). Like all humans, Muslims sin and fall short of God's glory (Rom. 3:23). Like all humans, God loved them so much that He sent His Son, so that those who believe in Jesus will have eternal life (Jn. 3:16).

2. *God calls Muslims to Himself!* God designed all of us to seek after Him. That includes Muslims. "From one

man, He made every nation of men, that they should inhabit the whole earth," God did this so men would seek Him and perhaps reach out to Him and find Him, though He is not far from each one of us. For in Him we live and move and have our being" (Acts 17:24-31, especially 26, 30). Like you and I, God has placed "eternity in their hearts" (Ecc. 3:11).

3. *Muslims are our neighbors.* No matter where they are, the overwhelming majority of Muslims are peace-loving, hospitable people.

4. *Muslims are people, too!* Most Muslims are concerned about the same things as you and me. They want to raise their children well. They are concerned about rising crime and pornography, and work hard to pay their bills and survive. Like us, human suffering and violence between peoples sadden most Muslims. Many Muslims yearn for peace, friendship, and a happy life. We share the same concerns and needs.

5. *God is at work among Muslims!* Many Muslims are sensitive to God and spiritual things. Muslims often speak of how God appeared to them through dreams and visions, just like He did to the "God-fearing" Cornelius (Acts 10:1-8). There are many stories of healings because of God's power through Jesus. An increasing number of Muslims are hungry to know about God's dramatic work through Jesus.

6. *We are spiritually related.* Many Muslims look to 'Ibrahim' (Abraham) as "our forefather" (Rom. 4:1).

Since those who follow Jesus call Abraham "the father of all who believe" (Rom. 4:11), that makes us 'cousins'! Like us, Muslims believe in one true God, the Creator of all peoples.

7. *Muslims value our Holy Book and Jesus*. The Qur'an specifically commends the *Taurat* (books of the Law, the first five books of the Bible); the *Zabur* (the Psalms, or wisdom literature); and the *Injil* (the Gospels). According to the Qur'an, Jesus was sent by God to earth, Jesus healed many during his ministry; and he is returning to judge the living and the dead.

8. *Muslims have something to teach us*. Muslims take the spiritual world very seriously and generally are more open to discuss spiritual issues. They have a very high respect for God and His power. Muslims place a high value on community and loyalty. Hospitality is very important to them.

9. *God made promises to their ancestors*. God made this promise to Ibrahim (Abraham): "As for Ishmael, I have heard you; behold, I will bless him, and I will make him fruitful, and I will multiply him. He shall become the father of twelve princes, and I will make him a great nation" (Gen. 17:20). God fulfilled this promise, for there are over one billion Muslims in the world today!

10. *God promised that Muslims who follow Jesus will be part of the multitude who are gathered about the throne of God*. When God gathers all His people at

the end of time, there will be representatives from every people group on the earth, "from every nation and tribe and people and language, standing before the throne and before the Lamb, clothed in white robes...crying out in a loud voice, 'Salvation to our God who sits on the throne'..." (Rev. 7:9-10).

Seven Old but Good Principles

Henry Martyn (Chapter 4) was a quick learner in sharing his faith with Muslims. He realized that public debate with Muslim scholars (Raymund Lull's method) was not effective. He developed some principles in 1810 that many today consider helpful in witnessing to Muslims:

1. Share your own personal experience: your testimony of how you experienced the forgiveness of sins and peace with God through Jesus Christ.
2. Look for good qualities in your Muslim friend and his culture.
3. Keep your message Christ-centered as you talk about the grace of God.
4. Encourage your Muslim friend to study the Bible so that he can discover the truth for himself.
5. Be a friend and encourager as your Muslim friend goes through this time of investigation and decision-making.
6. Minister to people's physical needs to help demonstrate God's love.
7. Trust the Holy Spirit to work in your Muslim friend.

Other helpful suggestions and principles are as follows:

1. **Be constantly in prayer.**
2. **Invite them to your home.** Muslims place a high value on hospitality. You would not leave a Muslim home without being offered something to drink, no matter how short the visit. Do the same with your Muslim friends. Ask beforehand about any dietary restrictions. Assume that your Muslim visitors will neither eat pork nor use alcoholic beverages.
3. **Be sensitive to Muslim moral values.** In Muslim cultures, friendship between a man and woman who are not related is rare. Your witness will be more effective with Muslim friends of your gender. Also, modest dress and behavior will help your new friend see that the behaviors they see in American media are not typical of all Christians.
4. **Learn the basics of their beliefs.**
5. **Listen and seek to understand.** Ask about their homeland, their customs and their religion—and listen with the same openness that you want from them. Remember that Muslims, as Christians, may vary in their individual beliefs and faithfulness to Muslim practices. Ask your new friend what his or her religion means personally.
6. **Welcome open and honest discussion of your different religions.** Many Muslims enjoy discussing their beliefs and how they differ from other religions. But remember that tearing down Islam is not your

goal. Instead, share the basic doctrines of your Christian faith, especially Jesus' role in assuring your salvation and enabling you to establish a personal relationship with God.

The Cost of Following Christ

"If anyone would come after me, he must deny himself and take up his cross daily and follow me. For whoever wants to save his life will lose it, but whoever loses his life for me will save it" (Lk. 9:23-24). The disciples in Jesus' day knew exactly what these words meant. Disciples who come out of Islam also understand; their decision to follow Christ may cost them everything, even their life.

The "Law of Apostasy" which is taken from the Qur'an and the *Hadith* teaches that Muslims who change their religion should be killed. This "Law" in Islam, according to Don McCurry, is "probably the single reason why more Muslims do not become Christians." (McCurry 2001:294) Religious freedom to "Orthodox Muslims" means that others are free to become Muslims, but Muslims are not free to change their religion. When they dare to come out of Islam, they may be disowned by their family, fired from their jobs, or thrown out of their universities. If they are married, their wives and children may be taken away from them. In general, they become outcasts.

Contextualization (Culture Friendly)

In order to see the gospel spread among Muslims, great care must be taken to allow Muslims to follow Christ and remain in their culture. This idea of contextualization is not new. The apostle Paul presented the gospel differently to the men of Athens than he did to the Jews. The apostle Paul said, "Though I am free and belong to no man, I make myself a slave to everyone, to win as many as possible. To the Jews I became like a Jew, to win the Jews...To those not having the law (Gentiles) I became like one not having the law, so as to win those not having the law" (1 Cor. 9:19-21). Paul also helped the other early believers realize that a Gentile did not have to become a Jew in order to follow Christ. This, too, is the issue that must be dealt with by the friends of Ishmael; do Muslims have to turn their back on their own culture and customs in order to follow Christ? Does Christianity have to be seen as a western religion? In the Philippine context, does a Muslim have to become a "Visayan" or "Christianos" in order to follow Christ?

Many mistakes have been made in the past in the method used to witness to Muslims. Some of the "Old Friends of Ishmael" included in this book made mistakes. We can learn from their commitment, but do not need to follow all of their methods. Most early missionaries presented the gospel, using a traditional church approach (C1, C2, and C3). This may be one reason there were few converts and those who did follow Christ, left or were removed from their culture. They became outcasts not because of the gospel, but because of the form in which the gospel was presented. In recent years, missionaries have attempted more reasonable and sometimes "radical" approaches (C4, C5, and C6). Much discussion and debate has taken place about which approach is correct. Many cross-cultural workers feel most comfortable with the C3 and C4 model.

C1 Model: Traditional church using non-indigenous language.

Christian churches in Muslim countries are removed from the culture. Christians exist as an ethnic/religious minority.

C2 Model: Traditional church using indigenous language.

Church uses indigenous language, but in all its cultural forms is far removed from the broader Islamic culture.

C3 Model: Contextualized Christ-centered communities using Muslim's language and non-religiously indigenous cultural forms

Styles of worship, dress, etc. appear "Muslim." May meet in a church or more religiously neutral location. Majority of congregation is of Muslim background and call themselves Christians.

C4 Model: Contextualized Christ-centered communities using Muslim's language and biblically allowed cultural and Islamic forms.

Similar to C3 except believers worship looks like Muslim worship, they keep the fast, avoid pork and alcohol, use Islamic terms and dress. Community is almost entirely of Muslim background. Though highly contextualized, believers are not seen as Muslims by the Muslim community. Believers call themselves "followers of Isa Al-Masih," Jesus the Messiah.

C5 Model: Christ-centered communities of "Messianic Muslims" who have accepted Jesus as Lord and Savior.

Believers remain legally and socially within Islamic community. Aspects of Islam that go against the Bible are rejected or, if possible, reinterpreted. Believers may remain active in the mosque. Unsaved Muslims may view C5 believers as deviant and may expel them from the Islamic community. If sufficient numbers permit, a C5 "Messianic mosque" may be established.

C6 Model: Small Christ-centered communities of secret/underground believers

Isolated by extreme hostility, usually individual believers but sometimes in small groups. Believers typically do not attempt to share their faith, others suffer imprisonment or martyrdom.

Two Christian workers in a very closed Islamic country share what they did in their C4 approach. Even though they did not see many Muslims come to faith in Christ, they were accepted by the community and had many opportunities to share the gospel.

1. They adopted Muslim names.
2. They called themselves *Isayi*. (This was a culturally accepted term meaning "the one who follows Jesus")
3. They used the standard greeting, "Assalamu alaikum" and the response "Alaikum salam," and made a vocabulary change in using biblical words: Jesus= *Isa*; God = *Allah*; Church = *Jamaat*; New Testament = *Injil*; Old Testament = *Torah*; Psalms = *Jobur*
4. They wore national dress and adopted national grooming (long hair for women, and a beard for the men).
5. They did not eat pork or drink wine.
6. They worshiped using Muslim forms of prayer (kneeling, palms out, etc.)
7. They occasionally went to the mosque for worship.
8. They participated in the month-long fast of Ramadan.
9. They attended Muslim festivals.
10. They learned to handle and respect the Bible as Muslims do the Qur'an. For example, they would kiss the Bible when reading it in the presence of a Muslim.

Is there only one method?

What would Jesus do? How would Jesus witness to a Muslim? Well, it just depends. Jesus never followed a method. He rarely did things the same way twice, because people and their needs are different. To the hardened Pharisees, Jesus showed no mercy. However to Nicodemus, he took time to explain spiritual truths (Jn. 3). To the brokenhearted, Jesus gave forgiveness. Jesus loved the rich young ruler, but would not compromise. From the Orthodox Jew to the government rebel, Jesus knew how to present the message of the kingdom of God.

In the same way, we must focus more on people than a method. In each of the five major groups of Muslims, there are characteristics and bridges, which can be used to help us be more effective in sharing the gospel.

The Sunnis. They want to live under the *Shariah* Law. This type of Muslim would be very similar to the Orthodox Jew of Jesus' day. The Sunni labors to keep the law in order to be saved. Jesus would patiently show the Sunni that the law kills. There is no salvation through the law. There must be a substitute to die for us. Chronological storytelling could possibly be an effective method.

The Shias. Shias believe that "Divine Light" indwelt Muhammad. They believe that Husayn (martyred at Karbala in AD 680) died for his people. This event is re-enacted every year with passion plays. Shiism has always been a protest movement within Islam. Jesus must be presented as the "Light of the world." Shiite Muslims are incredibly receptive when they see the suffering of Jesus acted out, for example, in the Jesus film.

The Sufis. They are seeking after the inner experience. They have an emphasis on dying to self. Sufis' concern is love for God, repentance, and turning away from the world. Sufis tend to meet in small groups. Prayer and possibly power encounters; use of chronological storytelling, and house churches might be possibilities among this group.

Folk Muslims. Folk Muslims need healing, deliverance, forgiveness, guidance, comfort, strength, and protection. They are looking for power. Christians must answer the questions they are asking. Power encounters through healing and deliverance, truth encounter through storytelling, and community through house churches or other contextualized worship are suggested strategies. Community development and other human needs type projects have proven effective with folk Muslims.

Militant Muslims. The question they are asking is "What went wrong?" "Why is Islam not dominant in the world?" Don McCurry says there are two different groups of militant Muslims. One group is really concerned about the needs and hurts of their people. The other group is just focused on power. For the first group, Christians have much to offer in showing true Christian love through community development type ministries. To those Muslims who think they are doing good by their violence, Jesus would say as He did to Peter, "Put your sword back in its place..." (Mt. 26:52) There is a better way.

God is moving among Muslims! "More Muslims have come to Christ in the past two decades than any other time in history. In North Africa, more than 16,000 Berbers have turned to Christ. In Kashmir, 12,000 Muslims turned from Jihad to the Prince of Peace." (Garrison 2004:99) There are reports of healings, miracles, dreams, and visions. God is moving among Muslims! But do not forget that where God has performed miracles; where God has brought about a harvest; where God is working among Muslims, His people are working there, too. God has never changed His method. He uses people. "How, then, can they call on the one they have not believed in? And how can they believe in the one whom they have not heard? And how can they hear without someone preaching to them?" (Rom. 10:14). Ishmael waits! Be a friend by sharing your life and by sharing the gospel.

13

The Unfinished Task

Almost a hundred years ago, Robert Speer said these words:

> The Church must wake up to her duty toward Islam. The evangelization of the world in this generation is the call of Jesus Christ to every one of His disciples to die to himself, and walk in the footsteps of Him who, though He was rich, for our sakes became poor, that we through His poverty might be rich, himself to count his life as of no value, that he may spend it as Christ spent His for the salvation of the world. (Wilson 1952:76) (Zwemer 1943:213)

Seventy years ago, Samuel Zwemer called for Christians to carry the good news to the most neglected and difficult fields. The call still goes out today! Islam is our greatest challenge and opportunity. As you read these statistics, do not forget that these numbers represent individuals who have eternal souls. May your burden grow to "pray to the Lord of the harvest." May God give you compassion on these "who have no shepherd." May your eyes be lifted up to see the harvest. Finally, may you hear God's call and bring His blessing to the sons of Ishmael. Will you be a friend to Ishmael?

(These statistics are taken from Appendix A of *Healing The Broken Family of Abraham*. As noted by Don McCurry, many of these numbers are approximations. In many countries, a census has not been taken for years. As I researched from different sources, I discovered that there are differences among the sources. Therefore I have decided to use Don McCurry's findings. It should be noted that some estimate the Muslim population at present to be around 1.3 billion.)

ASIA

Country	Percent Muslim	Muslim Population
Indonesia	82.9%	171,935,000
India	14.0%	138,418,000
Pakistan	96.7%	137,217,000
Bangladesh	87.0%	107,358,000
China	2.4%	29,820,000
Afghanistan	99.0%	24,552,000
Uzbekistan	68.2%	16,436,000
Russia	8.7%	12,780,000
Malaysia	55.0%	12,210,000
Kazakstan	40.0%	6,240,000
Azerbaijan	80.0%	6,160,000
Philippines	8.0%	6,024,000
Tajikistan	82.3%	5,020,000
Turkmenistan	76.0%	3,572,000

Kyrgyzstan	60.0%	2,820,000
Thailand	4.0%	2,444,000
Myanmar	3.8%	1,790,000
Sri Lanka	7.8%	1,474,000
Georgia	21.3%	1,150,000
Nepal	3.5%	830,000
Singapore	15.4%	601,000
Cambodia	2.9%	313,000
Maldives	99.4%	298,000
Japan	0.2%	253,000
Brunei	71.0%	213,000
Vietnam	0.2%	157,000
Armenia	3.3%	125,000
Taiwan	0.5%	109,000
Mongolia	4.0%	96,000
China, Hong Kong	1.0%	67,000
Laos	1.0%	53,000
Bhutan	5.0%	40,000
South Korea	0.06%	28,000
Total		**690,603,000**

OCEANIA

Country	Percent Muslim	Muslim Population
Australia	1.5%	281,000
Fiji	7.5%	60,000
Total		**341,000**

THE MIDDLE EAST

THE ARAB MIDDLE EAST WITHOUT NORTH AFRICA

Country	Percent Muslim	Muslim Population
Iraq	95.4%	20,797,000
Saudi Arabia	93.4%	18,867,000
Yemen	99.9%	15,784,000
Syria	90.5%	14,118,000
Jordan	94.0%	4,324,000
Oman	95.5%	2,388,000
United Arab Emirates	84.6%	2,284,000
Lebanon	53.0%	2,173,000
Kuwait	89.9%	1,708,000
West Bank	82.1%	1,478,000
Gaza	98.0%	1,078,000
Israel	14.5%	870,000
Bahrain	85.0%	510,000
Qatar	91.4%	457,000
Total		**86,836,000**

NORTH AFRICA

Country	Percent Muslim	Muslim Population
Egypt	85.4%	55,937,000
Algeria	99.4%	30,019,000
Morocco	99.8%	27,645,000
Sudan	70.0%	19,950,000

Tunisia	99.5%	9,453,000
Libya	96.0%	5,472,000
Total		**148,476,000**

Total Arab World (Middle East and North Africa)
235,312,000

NON-ARAB MIDDLE EASTERN COUNTRIES

Country	Percent Muslim	Muslim Population
Turkey	99.8%	64,670,000
Iran	99.0%	63,459,000
Cyprus	22.0%	154,000
Total		**128,283,000**

Total for All Middle East and North Africa
363,595,000

SUB-SAHARAN AFRICA

Country	Percent Muslim	Muslim Population
Nigeria	40.0%	48,720,000
Ethiopia	35.0%	20,440,000
Tanzania	35.0%	10,710,000
Somalia	99.96%	10,696,000
Niger	90.5%	9,141,000

Mali	86.3%	8,716,000
Senegal	90.8%	8,172,000
Guinea	83.1%	6,233,000
Cote d'Ivoire	38.7%	6,037,000
Burkina Faso	48.0%	5,424,000
Cameroon	24.0%	3,432,000
Chad	45.5%	3,367,000
Ghana	16.0%	3,024,000
Mauritania	99.7%	2,493,000
Mozambique	13.0%	2,418,000
Sierra Leone	43.1%	1,983,000
Eritrea	51.0%	1,938,000
Kenya	6.0%	1,698,000
Uganda	8.0%	1,680,000
Malawi	14.5%	1,421,000
Gambia	95.4%	1,145,000
Togo	21.0%	1,029,000
Benin	17.0%	1,020,000
Rwanda	10.0%	800,000
Dem. Rep. Of Congo	1.4%	686,000
Djibouti	94.6%	662,000
Comoros	98.0%	490,000
South Africa	1.25%	486,000
Guinea-Bissau	44.0%	484,000
Liberia	13.3%	372,000
Madagascar	2.2%	308,000
Zimbabwe	1.6%	176,000
Mauritius	12.5%	150,000

Central African Republic	3.3%	112,000
Zambia	1.0%	95,000
Burundi	1.0%	55,000
Gabon	4.2%	50,000
Congo	1.3%	35,000
Reunion	4.2%	29,000
Total		**165,927,000**

Total North Africa
148,476,000

Total for All of Africa   *314,403,000*

EUROPE
EASTERN AND SOUTHERN EUROPE

Country	Percent Muslim	Muslim Population
Yugoslavia	17.0%	1,802,000
Bosnia-Herzegovina	40.0%	1,600,000
Albania	40.0%	1,320,000
Bulgaria	13.9%	1,154,000
Italy	1.9%	1,096,000
Macedonia	25.0%	500,000
Spain	0.77%	303,000
Ukraine	0.47%	236,000
Romania	1.0%	225,000

Country	Percent Muslim	Muslim Population
Croatia	5.0%	210,000
Greece	1.5%	158,000
Belarus	0.2%	20,000
Estonia	1.0%	14,000
Hungary	0.1%	10,000
Latvia	0.4%	10,000
Total		**8,658,000**

WESTERN EUROPE

Country	Percent Muslim	Muslim Population
France	7.7%	4,528,000
Germany	2.5%	2,058,000
United Kingdom	2.5%	1,478,000
Netherlands	2.7%	424,000
Belgium	3.1%	316,000
Austria	1.4%	113,000
Switzerland	1.0%	71,000
Sweden	0.8%	71,000
Denmark	1.0%	53,000
Norway	0.5%	22,000
Portugal	0.2%	20,000
Total		**9,154,000**

Total for All of Europe
17,812,000

NORTH AMERICA

Country	Percent Muslim	Muslim Population
United States	1.8%	4,864,000
Canada	0.8%	245,000
Total		**5,109,000**

LATIN AMERICA

Country	Percent Muslim	Muslim Population
Argentina	1.5%	542,000
Brazil	0.1%	162,000
Panama	4.5%	126,000
Suriname	24.0%	96,000
Venezuela	0.4%	93,000
Trinidad-Tobago	5.9%	77,000
Colombia	0.2%	77,000
Guyana	9.0%	63,000
Mexico	0.03%	29,000
Total		**1,265,000**

Total for Western Hemisphere
6,374,000

World Total	**21.0%**	**1,244,652,000**

THE MUSLIM COUNTRIES OF THE WORLD

Listed below are 49 countries of the world that have at least 50% Muslim population. The total population of these countries is approximately one billion people or 77% of all the Muslim population. The countries are listed according to the actual size of their Muslim population, not the total population of the country.

Country	Percent Muslim	Muslim Population
Indonesia	82.9%	171,935,000
Pakistan	96.7%	137,217,000
Bangladesh	87.0%	107,358,000
Turkey	99.8%	64,670,000
Iran	99.0%	63,459,000
Egypt	85.4%	55,937,000
Nigeria	40.0%	48,720,000
Algeria	99.4%	30,019,000
Morocco	99.8%	27,645,000
Afghanistan	99.0%	24,552,000
Iraq	95.4%	20,797,000
Sudan	70.0%	19,950,000
Saudi Arabia	93.4%	18,867,000
Uzbekistan	68.2%	16,436,000
Yemen	99.9%	15,784,000
Syria	90.5%	14,118,000
Malaysia	55.0%	12,210,000

Somalia	99.96%	10,696,000
Tunisia	99.5%	9,453,000
Niger	90.5%	9,141,000
Mali	86.3%	8,716,000
Senegal	90.8%	8,172,000
Kazakstan	40.0%	6,240,000
Guinea	83.1%	6,233,000
Azerbaijan	80.0%	6,160,000
Libya	96.0%	5,472,000
Tajikistan	82.3%	5,020,000
Jordan	94.0%	4,324,000
Turkmenistan	76.0%	3,572,000
Chad	45.5%	3,367,000
Kyrgyzstan	60.0%	2,820,000
Mauritania	99.7%	2,493,000
Oman	95.5%	2,388,000
United Arab Emirates	84.6%	2,284,000
Lebanon	53.0%	2,173,000
Sierra Leone	43.1%	1,983,000
Eritrea	51.0%	1,938,000
Kuwait	89.9%	1,708,000
Bosnia-Herzegovina	40.0%	1,600,000
West Bank	82.1%	1,478,000
Albania	40.0%	1,320,000
Gambia	95.4%	1,145,000
Gaza	98.0%	1,078,000
Djibouti	94.6%	662,000

Bahrain	85.0%	510,000
Comoros	98.0%	490,000
Qatar	91.4%	457,000
Maldives	99.4%	298,000
Brunei	71.0%	213.000
Total		**963,278,000**

14
Conclusion:
Stories of MBBs

The call of God to take the gospel to the sons of Ishmael must be obeyed by this generation. Jesus commands us to go! It should be the exception if we stay. The young person who considers himself hindered should be very sure that he has been hindered by the Holy Spirit, and not by friends, self, ambition, family, sin, or Satan. Jesus commands us to go! But the Church is busy at play feeling so called to stay. Are seekers of pleasure so many and seekers of souls so few? What the Church needs today are men and women and young people unwilling to stay.

The call of God to take the gospel to the sons of Ishmael must be obeyed by this generation. The reality of hell demands that we go. There are only two places that dead people go: heaven and hell. Those who do not have a relationship with Jesus Christ will spend eternity in torment. Somehow, this reality needs to move us to action. Could it be we really don't believe this anymore? Could it be this generation of young people is Universalists, believing that somehow everyone will make it to heaven?

A student told me of a conversation she had with an atheist. The atheist said, "If it is really true that Jesus is the only way and those who do not believe in Him go to hell, then what are you doing?" He continued, "If I believed that to be true, I would quit school, sell everything I have, and go everywhere telling people this news!" If only for a moment we could come close to the door of hell and hear the cries of those imprisoned forever, we would stop seeking great things for ourselves and would seek first the kingdom of God.

The call of God to take the gospel to the sons of Ishmael must be obeyed by this generation. The accomplishment and commitment of those in the past demand that we continue. Without technology, modern transportation, communication, and medical care, the early believers "preached the word wherever they went" (Acts 8:4). In the early part of the 20th century over 100,000 students pledged to "evangelize the world in this generation." One of those students, William Borden, gave up a great inheritance to be a friend to Ishmael. He died in Egypt at the age of 25. Found written in the front of his Bible were these words: "No reserves, no retreat, no regrets." The call of God is for young people to trade in their backpacks for crosses and follow the hard road, and if there is no road at all, then be willing to push ahead. Like those heroes of the past, if we must fall, let us make sure we fall on the battlefield, not the playground.

The call of God to take the gospel to the sons of Ishmael must be obeyed by this generation. The reality of the need demands that we go. About 1.3 billion Muslims have waited long enough! Are all of these in need of the Savior? Yes! Will all of these become followers of Jesus? Reality tells us no. Are all 1.3 billion eagerly waiting for a messenger to witness to them? Probably not. Are some in every land and every people group waiting? I believe they are. Numbers and statistics do not touch our hearts. But Paul was called to Macedonia when he had a vision of a man saying, "Come over and help us." If you have not been called yet by the clear command of Jesus, the reality of hell, the example of those in the past, may you hear God's call through the stories of Muslim Background Believers.

One day, Sami, a twelve-year-old Muslim boy in a North African country, bought a newspaper. In it, he read these words, "If you want to receive a Bible correspondence course and a Bible, write to this address." He did write the address, and without anyone knowing, Sami studied for two years. However, Sami says, "My cousin discovered that I was having correspondence with Christians. And he warned me that if the police discovered this, they would throw me in jail. I was just 14 years old and jail was something I feared. I stopped studying the Bible. But from that moment on I began to ask myself, 'Why do the people turn away and don't accept information concerning Christianity?'"

God would not give up on Sami. Several years later, through a radio program, he came in contact with a believer from Morocco. This was the first believer Sami had ever met. Sami was given a Bible. He began to study both the Qur'an and the Bible. He said, "I made comparisons between the two. And to tell you the truth, during this time I found myself in total confusion with no way to get out. The Qur'an said that it was the last and the only truth inspired by God. But on the other hand, the Bible said the same thing: Jesus said in John 14:6 that He was the only way to salvation. I was perplexed and I asked myself the question, "What is the TRUE way?"

Through reading the Bible, Sami came to the truth. He was now 21 years old. He said, "Before, I practiced the Islamic laws without being sure I would go to heaven. Furthermore, I did not know how I could fix the matter of my being separated from God because of my sin. I no longer need the Islamic pillars and more laws in order to please God and reach Him. Jesus Christ offered me pardon for my sins and the sins of others through his death on the cross."

Sara was born into a wealthy Shiite family in Iran. Her father was a very devoted Muslim man who loved to please God. He was spiritually sensitive and open to studying other religions, but according to Sara, "There was not a Christian who wanted to share deeply with him." Even though her father had trained with the U.S. military, and had lived in America on several occasions, "no one ever witnessed to him."

When Sarah was a teenager, she moved to America. After several years, she began to be drawn to Christianity by the peace and joy she saw in the lives of believers. She began to seriously search for the truth. She did not want to leave Islam. She prayed, "Allah, show me, in Islam, how I can be like them (joyful believers)." The answer never came. She continues, "I finished the Qur'an and begin to see that the God of the Qur'an and the God of the Bible were different. If Islam is right then Christianity cannot be right. Some one is telling a lie here! I would pray to God every night to show me the truth. I was suspicious of Islam now, with all of the hate, judgment, wrath, lies, ungodly life of the prophet, etc. I could not believe the Christian message that I needed a Savior, and that was Jesus Christ: God Himself! What a strange message! God, please show me which one is the truth?"

After several months of studying the Bible and attending church, Sarah was "BORN AGAIN." Many asked her what changed her mind? She gladly says, "God did. He is the answer and truth."

Suraj was born in an Islamic country, where Christianity was strictly forbidden. He says, "Growing up, I knew nothing about Jesus Christ." However, one day he was given a Bible. Suraj comments, "When I read it, I was surprised to find that God loved me and made a way to forgive my sins. I learned that Jesus Christ died on the cross. I could be saved and would not have to die for my sins. In studying Islam, I had not found the way to know God. In studying the Bible, I found that Jesus could satisfy my hunger for Him."

Bassam was raised in the Middle East. At the age of 18, he joined a radical Islamic group. He said, "I thought I was doing everything I could for God, as I knew Him. After a short time I started to get some training in using guns and making explosives. I wasn't very comfortable with what I was doing— hurting people for God's sake. I thought that either I, or the group, had misunderstood the teachings of God. I started to study the Qur'an and the Hadith all over again, to see what I had missed. After a couple of years I was amazed at what I found.

I found that Islam is not the peaceful path to God as I used to believe; on the contrary, it's so violent. If I have to establish God's will by any means possible, even by killing people, I said it cannot be the way to God. At this point, I never considered leaving Islam, yet I was sure that it was not leading me to God. I was so sad. Everything I had believed in was wrong. I started doing drugs, and stopped talking about God at all.

"Then I met a Christian who did not know much of the Christian theology but who was full of love for others. Even though a radical Muslim friend of mine threatened this Christian with death, this did not stop him from loving this man. I was surprised at this Christian's good character. Everything I had learned all my life about Christians, from my reading of Islamic writings and Muhammad's opinion, was very negative. I asked this friend if I could have a copy of the Bible. After starting to read the Bible, I found a very big difference between what is actually written in the Bible and what I had heard people (Muslims and even nominal Christians) say about it. I was really convicted by one thing in the Bible, namely the teaching that no one is righteous but Jesus. He was the highest example of a human being, one who really deserved to be followed. It took me some time until I finished the whole Bible. After about one year of hard struggle with myself, I decided that I wanted to follow God as He shows Himself in Christ.

"I prayed to Him and He was here. For the first time in my life I felt that God was here. I was so happy, and so sad. Happy to know He is here and sad for what I had missed. It felt very peaceful and I wanted this feeling to last forever. I still remember the very first time I prayed; I ran out of the room because for the first time in my life I felt the presence of God. I have been following Him since then."

Adewale's testimony is about the power of God to bring someone out of folk Islam. He was raised in western Nigeria. His father had four wives and was a *Haji*. Adewale's family had many witch doctors and 21 household gods. He remembers, "All through my years at Ijebu, I remember that it was one ritual after another: rituals to counter the negative ones that were being directed at us. There were relatives who died from these curses. My dad was killed from a curse. There were others whose lives were destroyed and became useless to themselves and to society. I was almost always in a spiritual battle. My mom was always taking me to witch doctors, both in and outside our area."

To gain power or combat evil, Adewale enrolled in an Islamic school. The Imams tried to help him get free from demonic power, but they could not. They advised him to pray more. He bought a booklet of the 99 names of Allah. Sometimes, all night, he chanted these names and other memorized prayers. Adewale says, "In spite of my renewed spiritual commitment, the problems with demons continued. I contemplated suicide twice. There was no hiding place from the demons. I remember one ritual of *obatala* (a Yoruba god). It was meant to appease those who were responsible for my problems. The witch doctor called my mom and told her that I must have done something terribly wrong against some people. This was after three hours of fruitless efforts at appeasement! This is usually the situation with Yoruba witch doctors. Whenever they encounter someone more powerful than them, they either give up or continue to take your money, even though they know there is nothing they can do for you."

In April 1994, Adewale read a book on how to counter the effects of curses and spells. It was written by a Christian. This book helped change his life. When Adewale confessed Jesus as Lord and Savior, his life changed. He said, "Members of my family could hardly believe it. I no longer need to go to witch doctors. Jesus Christ did it all. And without any ritual or sacrifice on my part!"

Kadir, from Algeria, met some Christians. Later, while thinking about killing himself, he heard a voice telling him to give his life to Jesus. He started reading the book of John. He says, "I understood I was a sinner and needed God in my life. I turned to Jesus, believing He died for me, was buried, rose again and is seated at the right hand of the Father in heaven. I prayed inviting Him into my life and I received Him in my heart as my personal Savior and Lord."

Leah was a devoted Muslim woman. She began to feel that there was something missing in her life and in her Muslim faith. She prayed, "Lord, show me if the Muslim faith is the truth." After this sincere prayer, she began to have dreams. In one dream she says, "I saw some Christians standing in line to get into heaven. I tried to get into this line also, but a very tall being blocked my path and I started to cry because the side I was on was really horrible, but the side they were on was a beautiful place, so beautiful, so blue."

Several months later, Leah met with some Christian ladies who explained the gospel. She has now become a follower of Jesus. Leah has faced terrible persecution. Her husband left her and she is not permitted to see her son. It has been very hard for her, but she says, "I have never regretted becoming a Christian." She now knows the truth: Jesus Christ.

Ali, a Kurd, was searching for God. He was searching for a new life. One day a group of people approached him and told him of God's love. They gave him a Bible and a tract explaining the gospel. When Ali opened the Bible for the first time, he read these words, "If anyone is in Christ, he is a new creation; the old has gone, the new has come!" He says, "The Holy Spirit just brought me to my knees. That morning, I accepted Jesus Christ as my personal Lord and Savior."

Is the spread of Islam unstoppable? Are Muslims unreachable? You should be convinced by now that the answer to these questions is "No!" Wherever the gospel is preached among the sons of Ishmael, they are coming to Christ. Billy Graham says that every heart wants a true relationship with God. Without Christ, people are lonely. Without Christ, people are guilty. Without Christ, people are afraid of death. Money and possessions cannot make people happy. People are not satisfied until they are reconciled with God, through His Son Jesus Christ.

A survey was done of 600 MBBs from 39 countries and 50 different ethnic groups. They were asked the question, "Why did you become a follower of Jesus Christ?" Their top answers were: A sure salvation, Jesus (they were drawn to Him, when they read of His life, miracles, death, resurrection, etc), the Bible (when they read it, they believed), their search for truth, dreams (some dreams lead them to believers, like the story of Cornelius in Acts 10, other dreams confirm the message they have heard or read), love (they were attracted by the love of God, and the love of believers), and a personal relationship with God (many Muslims do not feel they can come near to Allah).

Can you hear God calling you? Listen closely with your heart to this call for help from a very "hard" Muslim group in Asia. "All my life as a Muslim, I had been reading the Qur'an. Everyday I would pray, 'Lord, show me the way, show me the way.' Then I read the Bible verse, John 14:6, 'I am the way, the truth, and the life; no one comes to the father except through me…Yes, the gospel is slowly reaching my people. My people are not invulnerable. They are not unreachable. They are as vulnerable and reachable as I am." Will you be a friend to Ishmael?

Appendix

Basic Beliefs of Islam and Christianity Compared

Term	Christianity	Islam
Afterlife	Christians will be with the Lord in heaven (Phil. 1:21-24), in our resurrected bodies (1 Cor. 15:50-58). Non-Christians will be thrown into hell forever (Mt. 25:46).	There is an afterlife (Sura 75) experienced as either an ideal life of paradise for faithful Muslims or hell for non-Muslims and those Muslims whose works and faith were not good enough.
Angels	Created beings, non-humans, some of which fell into sin and became evil (Isa. 14:12-15; Jude 6). They are very powerful. The unfallen angels carry out the will of God (Heb. 1:4-14).	Created beings who serve God. Angels (*jinn*) were created from light.

Term	Christianity	Islam
Atonement	The death of Christ on the cross (1 Pet. 2:24) where His blood becomes the sacrifice that turns away the wrath of God (1 Jn. 2:2) from the sinner when the sinner receives (Jn. 1:12), by faith (Rom. 5:1), the work of Christ on the cross.	There is no atonement work in Islam other than a sincere confession of sin and repentance by the sinner (Sura 15:26-27).
Bible	The inspired Word of God (2 Tim. 3:16).	Respected word of the prophets, but the Bible has been corrupted through the centuries and is only correct if it agrees with the Qur'an.
Crucifixion	The death by which Jesus paid for the sins of the world. It is only through this sacrifice that anyone can be saved from the wrath of God (1 Pet. 2:24).	Jesus was not crucified, although it appeared that he was.
Devil	A fallen angel who opposes God in all ways. He also seeks to destroy humanity (Isa. 14:12-15; Ezek. 28:13-15).	Iblis, a fallen *jinn. Jinn* are not angels nor men but created beings with free wills (Sura 2:268; 114:1-6).

Term	Christianity	Islam
God	God is a Trinity of Persons: Father, Son, and Holy Spirit. The Trinity is not three gods in one god, nor is it one person who took three forms. God is the maker of heaven and earth, of all that is seen and unseen.	There is no other God in existence. God is known as Allah. Allah is one person. There is no other God in existence. He is the creator of the universe (Sura 3:191), sovereign over all (Sura 6:61-62).
Heaven	The place where God dwells (2 Chron. 30:27; Psa. 33:13-14; Mt. 6-9). Heaven is the eventual home of Christians, who are saved by God's grace (Phil. 3:20).	Paradise to Muslims, a place of unimaginable bliss (Sura 13:35; 15:45-48) where the desires of faithful Muslims are met (Sura 3:133; 9:38; 13:35; 39:34; 43:71; 53:13-15).
Hell	A place of torment in fire out of the presence of God. There is no escape from hell (Mt. 25:46).	Hell is a place of eternal punishment and torment (Sura 14:17; 25:65; 39:26), in fire (Sura 104:6-7) for those who are not Muslims (Sura 3:131) as well as for Muslims whose works and faith were not good enough (Sura 14:17; 25:65; 104:6-7).

Term	Christianity	Islam
Jesus	Second Person of the Trinity. He is the Word who became flesh (Jn. 1:1, 14). He is both God and man (Col. 2:9).	A very great prophet, second only to Muhammad. Jesus is not the Son of God (Sura 9:30), not divine (Sura 5:17, 75), and was not crucified (Sura 4:157).
Judgment Day	Occurs on the day of resurrection (Jn. 12:48) when God will judge all people. Christians go to heaven. All others go to hell (Mt. 25:46).	Occurs on the day of resurrection where God will judge all people. Muslims go to paradise. All others go to hell (Sura 10:53-56; 34:28). Judgment is based on a person's deeds (Sura 14:47-52; 45:21-22).
The Qur'an	The work of Muhammad. It is not inspired. It is not Scripture.	The final revelation of God to all of mankind given through the archangel Gabriel to Muhammad over a 23-year period. It is without error and guarded from error by Allah.

Term	Christianity	Islam
Muhammad	A non-inspired man born in AD 570 in Mecca where he started the Islamic religion.	The last and greatest of all prophets of Allah whose Qur'an is the greatest of all inspired books.
Resurrection	Bodily resurrection of all people, non-Christians to damnation and Christians to eternal life (1 Cor. 15:50-58).	Bodily resurrection, some to heaven, some to hell (Sura 3:77; 15:25; 75:36-40; 22:6).
Salvation	A free gift of God (Eph. 2:8-9) to the person who trusts in Christ and His sacrifice on the cross. He is our mediator (1 Tim. 2:5).	Forgiveness of sins is obtained by Allah's grace without a mediator. The Muslims must believe Allah exists, believe in the basic beliefs of Islam, believe that Muhammad is his prophet, and follow the commands of Allah given in the Qur'an.

Bibliography

Adeney, Miriam. *Daughters of Islam: Building Bridges with Muslim Women*. InterVarsity Press, Downers Grove, IL, 2002.

Bridges, Erich and Jerry Rankin. *Lives Given, Not Taken: 21st Century Southern Baptist Martyrs*. International Mission Board, SBC, Richmond, 2005.

Curry, Dayna, Heather Mercer, and Stacy Mattingly. *Prisoners of Hope*. Doubleday, New York, 2002.

Finnie, Kellsye M. *Beyond the Minarets: A Biography of Henry Martyn*. Christian Literature Crusade, Pennsylvania, 2004.

For the Love of the Muslims. Southeast Asia Development Brief, 1997

Garrison, David. *Church Planting Movements: How God is Redeeming a Lost World*. WIGTake Resources, Midlothian, VA, 2004.

Graham, Franklin. *Living Beyond the Limits*. Thomas Nelson Publishers, Nashville, 1998.

_____. *Rebel With A Cause: Finally Comfortable being Graham*. Thomas Nelson, Inc., Nashville, TN, 1995.

Hickman, Claude. *Live Life on Purpose*. Pleasant Word, Enumclaw, WA, 2003.

Hitt, Russell T. *Jungle Pilot*. Discovery House Publishers, Grand Rapids, 1959.

James, Sharon. *My Heart in His Hands: Ann Judson of Burma*. Evangelical Press, Durham, England, 1998.

Jesus, Benjamin de and Deboran Cowles. *A Man Sent from God*. CAMACOP Inc., 1986.

Love, Rick. *"Faces of Islam: A Christian Perspective."* Mission Frontiers, Dec. 2001.

Marshall, Paul, Roberta Green, and Lela Gibert. *Islam at the Crossroads: Understanding its beliefs, history, and conflicts*. Baker Books, Grand Rapids, 2002.

McCurry, Don. *Healing the Broken Family of Abraham: New Life for Muslims.* Ministries to Muslims, Colorado Springs, CO, 2001.

McDowell, Josh. *The Best of Josh McDowell: A Ready Defense.* Here's Life Publishers, Inc. San Bernardino, CA, 1990

McDowell, Josh and Don Stewart. *Handbook of Today's Religions.* Here's Life Publishers, Inc., San Bernardino, CA, 1983.

Nehls, Gerhard. *Islam: As it sees itself. As others see it. As it is.* Life Challenge Africa, Nairobi, Kenya, 1996.

Page, Jesse. *Henry Martyn: Pioneer Missionary to India and Islam.* Ambassador, Greenville, 2003.

Piper, John. *Desiring God: Meditations of a Christian Hedonist.* Multnomah Books, 1986.

_____. *Let the Nations Be Glad: The Supremacy of God in Missions.* Baker Books, Grand Rapids, 1993.

Robson, James. *Keith-Falconer of Arabia.* George H. Doran Company, New York, 1922.

Smith, James Bryan. *Rich Mullins: A Devotional Biography.* Broadman & Holman Publishers, Nashville, 2000.

Taylor, Dr. and Mrs. Howard. *Hudson Taylor in Early Years: The Growth of a Soul.* R & R Clark, Edinburgh, 1927.

Tucker, Ruth A. *From Jerusalem to Irian Jaya.* Academie Books, Grand Rapids, 1983.

Van Rheenen, Gailyn. *Communicating Christ in Animistic Contexts.* Baker Book House, Grand Rapids, 1991.

Wilson, J. Christy. *Apostle to Islam.* Baker Book House, Grand Rapids. 1952.

Zwemer, Samuel M. *Into all the World.* Zondervan Publishing House, Grand Rapids, 1943.

Acknowledgments

This book began as a dream to bring over a billion Muslims closer to my Asian friends who live in the mountains. I watched them week after week serve the Lord as unknown soldiers, sometimes walking several kilometers to take God's Word to their friends and relatives. Most of these friends of mine will never go on to higher education. They will never drive a car or own a big house. They will never have a library and even if they did, most of the books would not be in their dialect. So, to you my pastor friends, living along the river and in the mountains, I thank you for the inspiration to write this book.

Our lives over the past several years have been consumed with standing before a new generation, raising the flag, and leading the push to reach the unreached and hard to reach. We have walked with some of the most outstanding leaders of this generation. Summer teams 2004-2008, your zeal and obedience continue to push us on.

Many people helped with editing and adding to the English manuscript; my mother—Olivia the First, my brothers—Jenkins and Moon Joon. Thank you, Eddie and Jimmy, for translating the book into a local dialect. Rey, Bryan, Arceli, Richard, Jake and Jael, you guys are also appreciated for your time in reading and editing.

I want to thank Peter, Jennie, and Ken for checking the manuscript for accuracy and giving many great suggestions to improve its content and clarity. Special mention goes to Josil Gonzales who willingly agreed to write Rev. de Jesus' inspiring story, Terese and Carr for their precious encouragement to get the book published quickly, and Drs. Larry and Mark for getting the word out that this book now exists! I also thank Joy and the CSM staff for designing the book and making all the necessary finishing touches in the final phase of production.

I would like to thank my family—Olivia, John Boy, Erin, and Elisabeth—for sharing this journey of walking through open doors and living life according to the compass.

And to the God who sees, hears, and cares for the sons of Ishmael, may You receive all glory and honor and praise!

Luke Hollaway
March 2009